A HISTORY

of

Jewish

PLYMOUTH

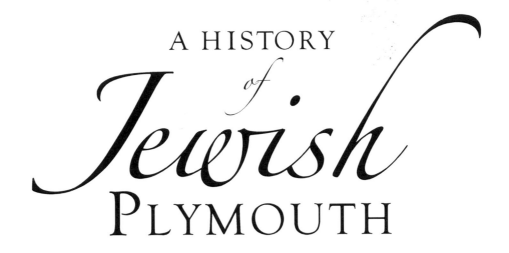

KARIN J. GOLDSTEIN

THE
History
PRESS

Published by The History Press
Charleston, SC 29403
www.historypress.net

First published 2013

Manufactured in the United States

ISBN 978.1.60949.511.4

Library of Congress CIP data applied for.

Contents

Preface

Plymouth, Massachusetts, America's Hometown, is located forty miles south of Boston. Each year several hundred thousand people visit to learn about the Pilgrims and America's heritage. Many climb the steps to Burial Hill to see monuments to the Pilgrims and may be surprised to find that Governor William Bradford's grave marker bears an inscription in Hebrew that reads, "The Lord is the help of my life." In the mid-1600s, Bradford taught himself the Hebrew language in order to read the scriptures as originally written. The Old Testament was very important to the Separatists who settled Plymouth. Indeed, many of the laws in early Plymouth and other New England colonies derive from Jewish law.

What visitors may not know is that Plymouth has had its own Jewish community for more than a century. Plymouth's synagogue, built in 1912–13, is located three blocks from Plymouth Rock. In the early twentieth century, Jewish immigrants lived in the oldest parts of Plymouth. They participated in Plymouth's economy as peddlers, shopkeepers and factory workers. They built a synagogue, homes and businesses, most of which are still standing today. While not as numerically significant as Italian or Portuguese immigrants to the town, Jews made important contributions to Plymouth's economy and culture.

Many works have been written about Jewish communities in urban areas, both large and small. This is not unexpected, as Jews tend to live in cities. Less has been written, however, about Jewish communities in towns.[1] Congregation Beth Jacob was established in 1909. While not the earliest

Jewish community on Massachusetts's South Shore, Plymouth's synagogue is one of the oldest in continuous use in the state and still hosts Shabbat services today.

This study examines the Jews who lived and worked in Plymouth. What part did they play in the development of twentieth-century Plymouth? How did they negotiate becoming American in the oldest colonial settlement in New England?

Acknowledgements

Plymouth's Jewish History Project started in 2001, when Bernard Resnick contacted Congregation Beth Jacob with the idea of researching the history of the Resnicks in Plymouth for a short book. Original project members included myself, Dr. Ray Russo and Vicki Blass Fitzgerald, as well as Rose Sherman Geller and the late Mitchell Toabe. Carl Finer and Dr. Barry Meltzer have made valuable contributions to the project as well.

The project took on a life of its own as I attempted to write an article on each of the families who helped to found the synagogue for the congregation's newsletter. Dozens of families contacted us, offering information, anecdotes and photographs. While I was not able to write about every family, a picture of courage, hard work and community began to emerge. The sum—a community history—was even more interesting than the individual family articles.

I'd like to thank my mother, for her patience in listening to endless stories about people she'd never met; Bruce Arons; Jim Baker; Jeremy Bangs; the late Morris Bloom; Ben Cohen and Debbie Cohen; Donna D. Curtin; Ina Zall Cutler; Nancy Kabelsky Cutler; Ginny Emond Davis; Susanne Taub Dubroff; Carl and Sheila Finer; Bill Fornaciari; Rose Sherman Geller; Eunice Dezorett Glassberg; David-Marc Goldstein; Meredith Hoffman; Melvin Klasky; Carolyn Sadow Leshin; Sandy Lipset; Norman Orent; Milton Penn; my colleagues at Plimoth Plantation, including Richard Pickering, John Kemp and Vicki Oman; Plymouth

Public Library, particularly the late Lee Regan for her support of local history; Bernard Resnick and Laura Resnick Altman; Karen and Stephen Resnick; Gladys Cohen Rotenberg; Dr. Ray Russo; Bernard and Leon Sadow; Allan Sherman and Susan Sherman Stone; Robert Shiff; Rabbi Laurence Silverman and Congregation Beth Jacob; the late Louis Stein; Muriel Swartz; Eugene Taubel; Joan M. Tieman; Rollene Waterman; Lawrence Winokur; Stephen and Jackie Keller Winokur; Leila Wolfe; and anyone I might have inadvertently left out.

When I first started this project, the late Mitchell Toabe told me, "What you write down is going to become the history, so you might as well get it right." I hope I did, and any errors remain mine.

Chapter 1

The Pilgrims and the Jews?

T he Jews are the first Pilgrims in history…they crossed the Euphrates river to escape from tyranny and oppression," stated Boston Reverend Dr. P. Israeli at the dedication of Plymouth's Congregation Beth Jacob synagogue in 1913. While it might seem strange to have a Jewish house of worship in America's first Puritan town, the Pilgrims had a special respect for the Jewish religion. Considering the importance of the Old Testament to the New England colonists, perhaps it is fitting that forty Jewish families, in their own way pilgrims seeking a new life in America, should settle in Plymouth and establish a congregation almost three hundred years after the Pilgrims landed on Plymouth Rock. Who were those early colonists, and what relation did they have to Jews and Judiasm?[2]

THE PILGRIMS

The core group of English colonists who founded Plymouth Colony in 1620 was part of a much larger reformation that swept Western Europe in the sixteenth century. When Martin Luther posted his points for debate within the Catholic Church in 1517, he set in motion a reexamination of Christianity, stripping away centuries of traditions to reveal the kernel within. The protesters, or Protestants, objected to various practices, including the church hierarchy, the concept of earning salvation and other traditions that had evolved since Christianity was established. They objected to the fact that the Bible was inaccessible to most of the population, who could not read Latin. While there were earlier translations of the Bible, such as that of John Wycliffe, they were based on the Latin version. The desire to study the Bible in its original languages stimulated an interest in ancient tongues, as clerics began reexamining the Old and New Testaments and the psalms. By the 1540s, Hebrew was taught in England at Cambridge and Oxford Universities. In Geneva, French theologian John Calvin and his followers translated the Bible from the original Hebrew, publishing the Old Testament in 1560.

The Reformation began in England in the 1530s, when King Henry VIII clashed with the pope over divorcing his first wife, Catherine of Aragon. The Church of England replaced Catholicism as the state religion in 1534. While the Church of England did use a liturgy translated into English, it kept in place the hierarchy of bishops. Instead of the pope, King Henry became head of the church. Although Henry VIII had addressed some of the issues of the Reformation, many clerics felt that his reforms had not gone far enough in purging the Church of England of Catholic traditions not mentioned in the Bible.

Reformers gained more ground during the reign of Henry VIII's son, Edward VI, but suffered setbacks when his eldest daughter, Mary I, ascended to the throne in 1553 and reestablished Catholicism. Many Protestant reformers were imprisoned or even executed for heresy. Others sought refuge in Continental centers of Reformed Christianity like Geneva and Amsterdam. Upon Mary's death, her sister Elizabeth became queen and reestablished the Church of England. According to the 1559 Act of Uniformity, citizens were required to attend the established church and use the official liturgy. Reformers who wanted to continue purifying religion of Catholic additions were known as Puritans. One of these was Robert Browne of Cambridge University, who felt that the Church of England could not be reformed adequately from within and advocated separating from it. Those who agreed with Browne became known as Separating Puritans, or Separatists. The Separatists did not want to worship in the established church and refused to use the official Book of Common Prayer, preferring to study the Bible itself, using the new Geneva translation.

One Separatist was William Brewster, a diplomat and postmaster who had studied at Cambridge University, a center of religious debate. He was exposed to Separatist ideas at services led by Robert Clyfton, who preached in Babworth, Nottinghamshire, and Brewster soon joined a Separatist congregation in nearby Gainsborough. While the English government under Queen Elizabeth I had looked the other way as long as dissenters attended official church services, King James I, who succeeded to the throne in 1603, was not as tolerant. James was funding an authorized translation of the Bible and did not tolerate nonconformists. When the Gainsborough congregation was harried by the government, Brewster invited it to worship at Scrooby Manor in Nottinghamshire, where he lived. Reverend John Robinson joined the group and later became the congregation's pastor. By 1607, Separatists in Scrooby and Gainsborough were in danger of arrest. A group led by Robinson decided to move to the Netherlands to take advantage of religious toleration to be found there. After one failed attempt when Brewster and his young protégé, William Bradford, were arrested and jailed, a group of Separatists managed to settle in Amsterdam in 1609.

The Netherlands won its freedom from Catholic Spain in 1581 and was one of the few countries in Europe that offered freedom of religion. Amsterdam in the early 1600s was filled with a bewildering array of religious groups: Reformed Christian sects, including the English Reformed and the Ancient Brethren; Huguenots (French Protestants); Walloons (Protestants from the south of Belgium); and Jews. Amsterdam's Jewish community had been established by the early seventeenth century. When the Separatists from Scrooby and Gainsborough arrived in Amsterdam, they moved into a poor area where many Jews from Spain and Antwerp lived. In Amsterdam, they met scholars like Henry Ainsworth, who translated the psalms from Hebrew. The Separatists worshiped with the English Reformed group, who met at the Beguinage Chapel, but the two English groups quarreled over doctrine. One argument involved whether it was right to hold worship in a building that had been used by Catholics or any people of other religions. When the Ancient Brethren mocked the English Reformed group for meeting in the Beguinage Chapel, as it had been Catholic, they responded that the Ancient Brethren were no better, as they met in a building formerly used as a synagogue.[3]

After a few months in Amsterdam's contentious environment, Pastor Robinson's group decided to move to a calmer place. They chose Leiden, a small city about twenty miles to the south, known for its university. Many well-known clerics and professors studied religion and ancient languages there, and Robinson and Brewster joined the religious debates. While Leiden did not have a Jewish community until the early eighteenth century, Hebrew was taught at the university, and it is not unlikely that Bradford and other Separatists were exposed to the language while there.[4]

John Robinson's group spent eleven years in Leiden, at which point they decided to settle someplace else. American schoolchildren learn that the Pilgrims left for America for religious freedom. This is not technically true—they had freedom to practice their faith in Leiden. Other issues contributed to their decision to leave the Netherlands. One problem was financial hardship. The Separatists, who had been farmers in England, were forced to find employment in urban Leiden. Many became textile workers but did not earn a lot of money. In his retrospective account *Of Plymouth Plantation*, Bradford lamented that their children had to work in order to make ends meet. Their economic situation in Leiden was so dire that Separatists from England were hesitant to join them. Another factor was the tenuous situation between the Netherlands and Spain. A treaty between the two nations was due to expire in 1620.

The Separatists applied to King James for permission to settle in America. In addition to being able to practice their religion, they also wanted a place where their children could grow up as Englishmen, away from the influence of the worldly Dutch. They applied to the Virginia Company of Plymouth (England) to settle in the northern parts of Virginia (around the Hudson River). Representatives were sent to England from Leiden to secure financial backing, ships and provisions. Merchant Robert Cushman went to Canterbury south of London, to arrange their voyage. He signed a lease for the ship *Mayflower* in rooms over a tavern on Palace Street, which, ironically, had been part of Canterbury's Jewry in medieval times.

Did any of the Pilgrims have Jewish heritage? Probably not. In their exhaustive early study of the Pilgrims, Henry Martyn Dexter and Martin Dexter mention a Mordecai Cohen. In April 1620, Separatist Thomas Rogers sold a house in Leiden to Cohen. A business transaction does not necessarily indicate that Cohen was a Separatist. Additionally, Pilgrim scholar Jeremy Bangs transliterated the entry as "Colven" rather than Cohen. Others have suggested that Leiden Separatist Moses Simonson, who arrived in Plymouth in 1621 onboard the *Fortune*, might have been Jewish. Both Moses and Mordecai are traditional Jewish given names, and there are Jews with the last name Simonson. Moses Simonson, however, is described by Edward Winslow as being the son of "a child of one that was in communion with the Dutch church in Leiden," so neither he nor his parents were practicing Jews. Additionally, Bangs notes that there are relatives of Simonson with Christian given names. In the seventeenth century, many Calvinists gave their children Old Testament biblical names.[5]

Did the Pilgrims know any Jewish people? They might have encountered some in Amsterdam, but only a couple of Jews were known to have lived in Leiden around that time. Technically there were no Jews in England—they had been expelled by King Edward I in 1190. A few Jews did live in cities like London and Bristol in the late 1500s, including Joachim Gans, a mining engineer who had been part of Sir Walter Raleigh's effort to colonize Roanoke Island in the 1580s. When the unsuccessful colonists returned to England from America in 1586, Gans moved to Bristol, where he taught Hebrew to those who wanted to study the Bible in its original language. When Cushman walked through Canterbury's former Jewry, he probably thought of Jews as a vanished people.[6]

Their voyage and finances arranged, in August 1620, a group from the Separatist community left Leiden for London and then America. Only the young and strong went, leaving small children and older people with Pastor Robinson, who intended to join them later. The next month, the Separatists were joined by other prospective colonists (many of them not dissenters), and two ships, the *Mayflower* and *Speedwell*, left Southampton for America. The *Speedwell* was not seaworthy, and after two attempts to repair it, the band left Plymouth, Devon, aboard a single ship—the *Mayflower*. After a sixty-six-day voyage, the *Mayflower* landed at what is now Provincetown, Massachusetts, in November with 102 people. In December 1620, the colonists decided to settle northward across the bay, in the Wampanoag village of Patuxet, which was deserted after its people had died from plague a few years earlier. The harbor had been named Plymouth by Captain John Smith in his 1613 map of New England.

NEW ENGLAND PURITANS AND LINKS TO JUDAISM

The Pilgrims were the leading edge of the thousands of English dissenters who settled in New England. In 1630, a group of Puritans led by John Winthrop founded the Massachusetts Bay Colony, forty miles north of Plymouth. Once in America, the subtle differences between Separatists and Puritans were less important—the Puritans in Massachusetts Bay had in fact separated themselves from the Church of England by moving to the colonies. Splinter colonies formed as ministers disagreed over doctrine. Thomas Hooker and his followers founded Hartford in present-day Connecticut in 1636 because he disagreed with Winthrop over who could be a member of the church. Roger Williams, who had been banished from Massachusetts Bay for his liberal ideas, founded Providence Plantations the same year in present-day Rhode Island, which became the only New England colony to welcome Jews.

Writings of the Pilgrims and Puritans reveal how they identified with the ancient Hebrews. The Puritans saw themselves as the Israelites, fleeing Pharaoh (the king) across the Red Sea (the Atlantic). According to scholar Peter Gay, "Like the children of Israel (whom the Englishmen admired as their spiritual ancestors, even if they would not have them in their midst), the English had erred in the wilderness and come at last into the promised land." *Mayflower* passenger and deacon Samuel Fuller wrote in a letter, "The Lord Jesus bless us and the whole Israel of God. Amen." The idea of the covenant as a solemn agreement between God and His people was another similarity between the Puritans and the Jews. The Mayflower Compact, signed in Provincetown Harbor in November 1620, can be considered such an agreement, as it states that they, "in the presence of God, and one another, covenant, and combine ourselves together into a civil body politic...for the general good of the colony." While Bradford referred to it as "an association and agreement," it was named "Compact" in the eighteenth century.[7]

Both Separatists and Puritans focused on the Old Testament as a primary source of true Christian values. The only holidays observed were those mentioned in the Bible—the Sabbath, days of fasting and humiliation and days of rejoicing. Christmas, Easter and other festivals that were part of the traditional English calendar were not celebrated. On December 25, 1621, Governor William Bradford ordered the colonists to work as usual, although some of the Anglican colonists protested. He agreed that "if they made it a matter of conscience, he would spare them until they were better informed." When Bradford returned at noon from working, he found them playing ballgames and other sports. "So he went to them, and took away their implements, and told them that it was against his conscience, that they should play and others work. If they made the keeping of it [a] matter of devotion, let them keep to their houses, but there should be no gaming or reveling in the streets."[8]

While many of the colony's laws derived from English common law, some were influenced by Mosaic law, particularly those regarding crime. When *Mayflower* colonist John Billington was found to have committed murder, Governor Bradford corresponded with Governor Winthrop of Massachusetts Bay. One of the justifications for executing Billington came from the scriptures. Bradford states that "the land [was] to be purged from blood," referring to Numbers 35:33, "nor can the land be purged from blood but by the blood of him that shed it." In another instance, a teenage boy,

Right: Memorial to Governor William Bradford, Burial Hill, Plymouth, Massachusetts. *Author photo.*

Below: Detail of Bradford's memorial stone, showing the Hebrew inscription. *Author photo.*

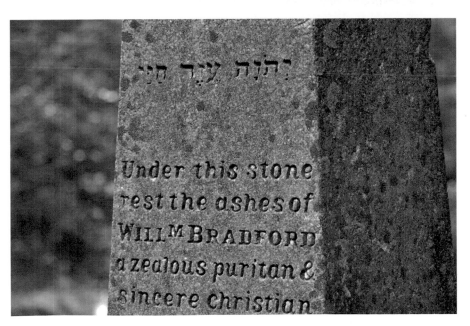

Thomas Granger of Duxbury, was found to have committed bestiality with several farm animals in 1642. Rape, sodomy and buggery were considered capital crimes in Plymouth Colony. In determining how to punish Granger, Bradford and his assistants turned to the Old Testament for examples. In accordance with Leviticus 20:15, Granger was hanged, and the animals were slaughtered and buried. In New Haven Colony's Code of 1655, half the laws contained Old Testament references. The Puritans tended to interpret the laws literally, without discussion, rendering them considerably more literal and strict than in Jewish tradition.[9]

As in other Puritan colonies, the Old Testament influenced Plymouth Colony laws regarding the Sabbath. Strict legislation about keeping the Sabbath was written in 1650. Prior to this, breaking the sanctity of the Sabbath was dealt with on a case-by-case basis. The new laws prohibited both working and traveling on the Sabbath, similar to Jewish law. Profaning the Sabbath in Plymouth Colony was punishable by a ten-shilling fine or by whipping, while the punishment for traveling on the Sabbath was twenty shillings.

Religious tolerance was *not* part of Plymouth Colony's laws. Not only is the idea that the Pilgrims came to America for religious freedom false, but so is the idea that they allowed freedom of religion in Plymouth Colony. In 1645, legislation was introduced in Plymouth's General Court to permit other religions. Bradford and other colony leaders, including Edward Winslow, were vehemently opposed, and Governor Bradford refused to let the proposition even come to a vote. With the 1650 laws, attendance at church, while practiced from the beginning, became mandatory in Plymouth Colony, and those who failed to attend were fined. Massachusetts Bay Colony was even more restrictive. In order to become a freeman and attain voting rights, a man had to be a member of the church. Those who preached against the official church could be banished, and four Quakers were executed for repeatedly returning from banishment to preach. The Glorious Revolution brought some tolerance to Massachusetts Bay by 1689 but only for Protestants. The 1780 Bill of Rights in the Massachusetts Constitution allowed freedom of worship, but Congregationalism remained the established religion in the state until 1833.[10]

BRADFORD'S HEBREW EXERCISES

In 1650, at the age of sixty-one or so, Governor Bradford began to teach himself Hebrew, the "Divine" language. His careful lettering and translations appear at the beginning of his account of Plymouth Colony's founding and growth, *Of Plymouth Plantation*, and in his 1652 *Third Dialogue*. He practiced both the Hebrew and Greek alphabets and transliterated individual words, including the names of God and the Hebrew words for heaven, stars and sun, man and woman. He transcribed phrases and verses from the Old Testament in Hebrew letters with English translations. As an older man nearing the end of his career, Bradford was writing a retrospective of how and why the colony was founded to inform and inspire the coming generation. Perhaps at this time in his life he allowed himself the luxury of taking time to study the original language of the scriptures. In his own words, "Though I am growne aged, yet I have had a longing desire, to see with my owne eyes, something of that most ancient languauge, and holy tongue, in which the law and oracles of God were write, and in which God, and angels, spake to the holy patriarchs of old time." Perhaps the phrase "The earth is full of ye mercie of Jehovah" from Psalm 33:5 had special meaning for Bradford as he recounted the history of the colony he helped to establish.[11]

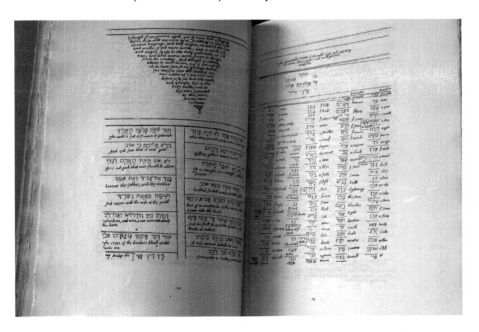

Detail of Governor William Bradford's Hebrew exercises from the front pages of the manuscript *Of Plymouth Plantation*, 1896 facsimile edition. *Courtesy of Plimoth Plantation.*

Jews in Colonial America

By the mid-seventeenth century, New England was composed of five colonies, four founded by reformed Christians influenced by the Old Testament. Many of the colonists identified with the ancient Israelites, having fled England across the Atlantic to the Promised Land. Many of their laws were based on Mosaic law, in particular the strict observance of the Sabbath. In spite of the Puritan respect for the Jews, only one of those colonies, Rhode Island, actually welcomed Jewish people. The Puritans liked the idea of the ancient Israelites more than the reality of their descendants.

The first Jews to arrive in the western hemisphere were Sephardic Jews (from the Iberian Peninsula) fleeing persecution from the Counter-Reformation. A group settled in Brazil in the 1630s. For a short time, the northeastern parts of Brazil were controlled by the Dutch, so Jews were tolerated. When the Netherlands began losing ground in the 1650s, many Jews moved to other Dutch colonies. A group from Recife arrived in New Amsterdam in 1654. While at first the governor of New Netherland, Peter Stuyvesant, was against letting them settle, his protests to the Dutch West India Company were overridden, as the company felt that Jews would be good for business.[12]

The earliest Jews who came to New England were also Sephardic. About fifteen families settled in Newport, Rhode Island, in 1658. As Rhode Island was religiously tolerant, they were able to form a community and established a burial ground in 1677. Although Jews were subject to restrictions in other New England colonies, there are occasional references to Jewish people in colonies other than Rhode Island. The first Jew recorded in Boston was Solomon Franco, who appears in a 1649 document. Jews also appear in the Hartford, Connecticut records, with a reference to "the Jews" in 1660.[13]

Several of the British colonies established later in the seventeenth century were more explicitly tolerant than the early settlements. The Carolinas were settled in 1670 by planters from Barbados—a colony of a colony. Philosopher John Locke was engaged to help write the colony's constitution, which specified tolerance, and Jewish families were among those who settled Charleston. Pennsylvania, founded by William Penn in 1681, also offered limited religious toleration, and Philadelphia had a Jewish community by the early eighteenth century. Nevertheless, there were very few Jews in early America—an estimate numbers them around just three hundred in 1700, a tiny proportion of the colonial population.[14]

The Pilgrims and the Jews?

Plymouth town and colony records have been thoroughly combed for information on the Pilgrims for more than a century and a half, but no mention of any Jewish people in Plymouth in the seventeenth or eighteenth centuries has yet been found. Early Plymouth did not have much to offer Jews. While hardly metropolises, Boston, Newport and Hartford were trading centers, with opportunities for merchants. Boston and Newport participated in trade with the West Indies, where many Jews lived. Although Plymouth was the seat of Plymouth Colony until 1691, it was much smaller in size and population than Boston. Additionally, its shallow harbor was poorly suited for large ships involved in international trade. After 1691, Plymouth became a shiretown, or county seat, rather than a colonial capital. While a legal center, Plymouth did not have the economic opportunities and cosmopolitan population of cities like Boston and Newport.

Chapter 2

Coming to America

MID-NINETEENTH-CENTURY JEWISH IMMIGRATION

Plymouth's population remained homogenous through the early nineteenth century. While a few people came from Great Britain in the eighteenth century, the vast majority of Plymouth residents descended from seventeenth-century Puritan immigrants. One of the first non-Protestant, non-English groups to arrive was the Irish. Irish laborers began migrating to Massachusetts in the early nineteenth century, and some found their way from Boston to Plymouth. Plymouth's nineteenth-century historian William T. Davis mentions the first Irishmen in town working for Judge Joshua Thomas, who helped them find a place of worship for their holy days. A Catholic service was held in Plymouth in 1849 at the Town House. While Plymouth became more religiously diverse in the early nineteenth century, there is still no mention of Jewish people.[15]

In the 1840s, a new wave of migration to New England began, which included Irish, German and Scandinavian immigrants. Refugees from potato blight, famine, poverty and political turmoil flooded Boston. Jews left various states in what is now Germany as early as the 1820s, continuing through the 1860s. Reasons included concerns about integration into German society after emancipation. Boston's first synagogue, Ohabei Shalom, was established in 1843, and the congregation established a Jewish cemetery in East Boston the next year. The majority of Boston's German Jews came from the northern provinces in and around Prussia.[16]

While thousands of immigrants stayed in Boston, a few trickled into Plymouth, attracted by economic opportunities. In the early nineteenth century, Plymouth was a thriving minor port that made its living from burgeoning industry and maritime trades. The abundance of streams and water power encouraged the development of industry as early as the 1790s, when a snuff mill was built on the Town Brook. By the second quarter of the nineteenth century, many industries worked hand in hand with seafaring. Iron mills made anchors, textile mills made sailcloth and ropewalks made rope. One of Plymouth's most significant businesses was the Plymouth Cordage Company, established by Bourne Spooner in 1824. Spooner visited New Orleans to study the rope industry and returned to his native Plymouth determined to make rope without slave labor. The Cordage Company opened in Seaside (North Plymouth), a couple miles north of Plymouth's town center. In order to attract labor, the Cordage Company solicited immigrants from central Europe, and many Germans came to Plymouth to work for the rope factory.

Among the German immigrants who worked as rope makers for the Cordage Company was Samuel Alexander, a Jew who lived with his wife, Caroline, in what is now North Plymouth. He and his family appear in Plymouth's 1860 and 1870 censuses, as well as in vital records. Three children are all listed at one time in town birth records, along with other immigrants living in North Plymouth. Apparently, several births from neighborhood families were reported to Plymouth authorities at the same time. The parents' place of birth is listed as Hesse. After staying in Plymouth a few years, the Alexanders moved to New York, where their descendants still live. They discovered the Plymouth connection when researching their family history. Interestingly, there are other Samuel Alexanders in the town's 1860 street directory who do not appear to be Jewish, as Yankees frequently used biblical given names. It is probable that other Jewish families came to Plymouth as part of the German migration.

At least one German Jewish family summered in Plymouth. Levy Mayer, a noted Chicago attorney, was born in 1858 in Richmond, Virginia. His parents were Bavarian Jews who came to America due to the many restrictions against Jewish people there. The Mayers left the war-torn South for Chicago, a prairie boomtown, in 1863. A talented student, Levy entered Yale at the age of sixteen and graduated from law school a few years later. He became a successful attorney who represented local business interests. Around 1900, Levy and his wife, Rachel, started spending summers in Plymouth.[17]

JEWISH IMMIGRATION TO PLYMOUTH, 1889–1913

A new wave of Jewish immigration to America began in the 1880s as part of a movement of people from Southern and Eastern Europe. These immigrants came from the Russian Empire, the Austro-Hungarian Empire and Romania. Unlike the few Jews who came with other Germans in the mid-1800s, the Eastern European immigrants came in large numbers— more than two and a half million between 1881 and 1924. Many were poor and unskilled and did not assimilate into American society as easily as the earlier arrivals. As a result of these factors, the Jews who came to America around the turn of the twentieth century had a very different experience than their earlier counterparts. Many lived in poor, overcrowded neighborhoods in cities like New York and Boston. A few found their way to towns like Plymouth.[18]

No one knows exactly which was the first of Congregation Beth Jacob's founding families to arrive in Plymouth. Louis and Ida Resnick came to Plymouth from Portland, Maine, with their son, Maurice, who was born in Portland in 1888. Their second child, Edith, was born in Plymouth on March 1, 1890. Ida Bahn Resnick's obituary states that she "was of the First Jewish Family in Plymouth." Louis's brother, David Resnick, arrived

Louis and Ida Resnick and family, circa 1914. *Back row, from left*: Joseph, Benjamin, Harry, Ida, Maurice; *front row*: Edith, Albert, Louis and Lillian. *Courtesy of the Resnick family.*

in New York in 1886, as seen in his naturalization certificate, but it is not known when he came to Plymouth—he may have come first. As shown by his naturalization certificate, peddler Joseph Berg lived on High Street in Plymouth in 1889. Other early families who came to Plymouth in the 1890s include the Orentlichers, the Sadows, the Toabes, the Medveds, the Julius Cohens and the Karnofskys.[19]

Plymouth's Jews came from a variety of places, although the majority came from the Russian Empire. A couple of families came from the Austro-Hungarian Empire and Romania. Those from Russia came from the "pale of settlement," a region on the western edge of Russia where Jews were allowed to live permanently. While "pale" comes from an Anglo-French word for "palisade," the Russian phrase *cherta osedlosti* means "line" as in "border." The pale included twenty-five *guberniyas* (administrative units), stretching north almost to the Baltic Sea, south to the Black Sea and west to the borders of Germany and Austria/Hungary. The pale included significant parts of Lithuania, Belorussia, Poland, the Ukraine and Moldavia, which were acquired by Russia as early as 1791.[20]

GUBERNIYA	FAMILY	CITY OR VILLAGE	COUNTRY TODAY
Chernigov	Dezoretts family	Buki	Ukraine
Galicia	Bass family	Jaworow	Austria
Grodno	Markus, Mayer	Bialystok	Poland
Kherson	Shriber family	Odessa?	Ukraine
Kiev	Cohen, Joseph	Cherepinka	Ukraine
Kiev	Zavalkovsky, Mendel	not known	Ukraine
Kovno	Frim, Harry	Krekenava?	Lithuania
Kovno	Kabelsky, Ida Snyder	Krekenava	Lithuania
Kovno	Miller, Harry	Kovno	Lithuania
Kovno	Resnick family	Krekenava	Lithuania
Kovno	Zavalkovsky, Edith Frank	not known	Lithuania
Lublin	Miller, Abraham	Hruszow	Poland
Vilna	Berg family	Olkeniki	Lithuania
Vilna	Pyzanski, Fannie Brody	Vilna area	Lithuania
Vilna	Sadow family	Doag	Lithuania
Volhynia	Cohen, Sylvia Rubinfein	Polona	Poland
Volhynia	Lewis family	Volochick	Ukraine
Volhynia	Orentlicher family	Starii Constantinov	Ukraine

Guberniya	Family	City or Village	Country Today
Volhynia	Sherman family	Dubno	Ukraine
Volhynia	Shoman family	Zazlov	Ukraine
Volhynia	Shwom family	Dubno?	Ukraine
Volhynia	Stein, Isaac	Varkovitch	Ukraine
Volhynia	Toabe family	Shepetovka	Ukraine
unknown	Besbris family	Alayka	Ukraine
unknown	Dretler family	Vanisla	unknown
unknown	Padlusky, John	Dalvin?	Russia
unknown	Sepet, Julius	Mar	Lithuania
unknown	Steinberg family	Zablockie	Poland

The Jews who settled in Plymouth came from six of the westernmost guberniyas in what are now Lithuania, Poland and the Ukraine. Several families came from Vilna guberniya, including the Bergs, Brodys and Sadows. The Resnicks came from the town of Krackenova (Krekenava) in Kovno guberniya, located in what used to be Poland, now Lithuania. The town had just over 1,500 Jews but was well known as a center for Torah study. Settlements ranged from the village of Doag (Daugi), which had only 511 Jews in 1900, to the city of Kovno (Kaunas), which was 35 percent Jewish, with more than 25,000 Jews in 1897. At least seven families came from Volhyniya guberniya farther south, particularly around Dubno, and a few were from near Kiev and Odessa.[21]

While the regions of origin in the pale run from north to south in a continuum, they were not the same culturally. When immigrants from these various regions came to America and settled together, they tended to associate with people from their same place of origin. Many communities split into Lithuanian *minyans* and Russian *minyans* (minimum of ten men needed to pray), as people from the different regions had different pronunciation, tunes, etc. Even in a small town like Plymouth, tension existed between the Lithuanians and Poles from the north and the Ukrainians/Russians from a bit farther south.[22]

Jews in the pale faced restrictive laws. They were only allowed to live permanently in towns and villages in the pale—several cities banned Jews from settling, and Jews were not allowed in agricultural areas. Jews made up more than 10 percent of the population but tended to be concentrated in towns and *shtetls*. Strict quotas meant that only a fraction of Jewish young people could attend school and college, even if the schools were half empty.

Only certain occupations were open to Jews—selling goods or working as artisans (i.e. tailoring). Lack of education and job opportunities meant that there were many people vying for the same work. The combination of the poor economic situation coupled with a dramatic population increase led to poverty. In some *guberniyas*, almost a quarter of the Jewish population needed financial assistance.[23]

A major incentive to emigrate for boys and men was conscription. While many Russians served in the army, the Jewish population was disproportionately hit with quotas. Jewish boys as young as twelve years old were drafted (and sometimes kidnapped) into the army for up to twenty-five years. They were forced to give up their religious practices. They had no access to kosher food, Jewish worship or study and were not allowed to speak Yiddish. The long terms of service encouraged Jews to leave their heritage and assimilate into Russian society.

Many Jewish families have stories about how their ancestors escaped Russia to avoid the draft, changing their names or even injuring themselves. Joan Tieman remembered hearing how her great-grandfather Joseph Berg broke his trigger finger to avoid conscription. (Another family member recalled that he cut the tendon in his finger.) Among the six Sadow sons who immigrated to the Boston area, some served in the Russian army and survived, while others escaped. At the age of thirteen, Max Sadow joined a group who secretly fled from their village of Doag, Lithuania. He arrived in New York in 1884 at the age of eighteen. Around the age of sixteen, Jacob Shiff was smuggled from his village of Dvinsk, Lithuania, to Hamburg and thus escaped to America. Another immigrant to Plymouth, Barnet Skulsky, was conscripted but survived his term in the Russian army.[24]

An important factor that sparked the mass migration of Jews from Russia was the assassination of Tsar Alexander II in 1881 by anarchist terrorists. The government blamed the Jewish people, among others, and encouraged mob violence (pogroms) against them. Pogroms included atrocities such as murder, rape, mutilation and kidnapping, as well as the destruction of homes and businesses. Particularly violent waves of pogroms broke out in the early 1880s, after the tsar was killed; in the early 1900s, in the wake of revolutionary activities; and after the 1917 revolution.[25]

The decision to emigrate was a major one. Passage was expensive, and families needed to save in order to afford to send the entire family. Frequently a father would immigrate to America and work for several years to raise enough money to bring over the rest of the family. Joseph Berg left Russia in

Joseph Berg, circa 1900. *Courtesy of Joan M. Tieman.*

the 1880s and worked for about ten years to afford passage for his wife and children. In other cases, young men like Max Sadow, Abram Sherman and Meyer Shwom came over on their own.

Would-be emigrants contacted a shipping line representative, who arranged the many stages of their journey. First they had to get a passport (sometimes provided by the agent) and then cross the Russian border, often staffed by corrupt soldiers. Many passed through Germany, where they were stopped at the border for medical exams to ensure that they did not spread diseases like cholera. From the German border, the emigrants boarded a train for a port, usually on the Baltic Sea (Hamburg, Bremen, Riga or Libau) or the North Sea (Antwerp or Rotterdam). Those who lived farther south often left from Odessa on the Black Sea.[26]

The vast majority of Jews fleeing Russia traveled to Hamburg to board oceangoing vessels. Often emigrants, already strapped for cash, had to wait for weeks for a ship. To provide them a place to stay, an emigrant village called the Veddel was built around the port. Up to five thousand emigrants at a time could await passage there. The Veddel featured a synagogue, an emigration hall, dormitories and a canteen with long tables. Kosher food was supplied by local German Jewish philanthropists.[27]

Passage could be direct (Hamburg straight to America) or indirect (Hamburg to England, then steamer to America). Kasiel Simon Bass, who arrived on Hamburg-America's *Furst Bismark* in 1894, sailed from Hamburg to New York via Southampton, England. Many emigrants chose the indirect route, probably because it cost less. They sailed from Hamburg to a port on the east coast of England, like Hull (Yorkshire) or Grimsby (Lincolnshire). From there they boarded a train to get to their steamship. While emigrant ships left Glasgow, Liverpool, London and Southampton, most sailing to Boston or New York in this period left from Liverpool. Several lines, including Cunard, White Star, Leyland and Dominion, sailed from Liverpool to Boston. Passage from Liverpool to Boston took eight to ten days. The length of the voyage varied, as often the route included other stops, like Queenstown, Ireland, or Halifax, Nova Scotia.[28]

Detailed passenger lists for the Steinberg family indicate that they took the indirect route. Jacob Steinberg arrived in America around 1899 and was able to send for his wife, Fannie, and two children in 1904. Fannie, with six-year-old Michel (?) and three-and-a-half-year-old Selig, left Lithuania for Hamburg, where they boarded the steam ferry *Oldham* on July 9. Like many boats that brought emigrants to the east coast of England, the *Oldham* was owned by a railway, which transported travelers to a west coast

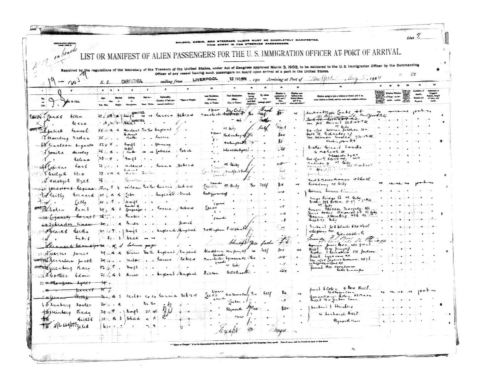

Passenger list of the SS *Carpathia*, Liverpool to New York City, July 26, 1904. The Steinbergs, Frady (Fannie), Michel and Zelik (Selig), are listed at the bottom of the page. Column 16 indicates that they were going to join Frieda's husband, Jacob Steinberg, who lived on Sandwich Street in Plymouth.

port. The ferry docked in Grimsby a few days later. The Great Central Railway, which operated the *Oldham*, ran a hostel for emigrants, where the Steinbergs might have stayed. A few days later they boarded a train for Liverpool and embarked on the Cunard liner *Carpathia* on July 25, arriving in Boston eleven days later. Their entire journey, from Lithuania to Boston, took twenty-seven days.[29]

Since England was a stop on the route to America, some families stayed or even settled there for a while. Sue Sadow was the daughter of Jewish immigrants to Plymouth. Her autobiography, *Can Do! Said Sue*, tells of life in Plymouth in the early 1900s. At least one family member, her uncle Jacob, settled in England when he left Lithuania. He lived in Manchester (near Liverpool) with his family for eighteen years. Many English cities, like Manchester, Leeds and London, had large Jewish populations. According to passenger lists, Morris Resnick and his wife, Celia, also spent several months in London before embarking for America.[30]

Immigrants who arrived in the 1880s and early 1890s most likely traveled steerage, the cheapest way of traveling. Steerage passengers traveled on the lower deck, in large sections rather than cabins or staterooms. Usually single men traveled in the forward section, married couples in the middle and single women at the back, supervised by a matron. Passengers slept in berths within each section and ate at long tables set up in the common space. The Toabe family traveled on Cunard's *Catalonia* in 1899. The ship was built in 1881 and was getting old. Its last transatlantic voyage occurred a few months after the Toabes sailed.[31]

Around the turn of the century, conditions onboard ocean steamers improved. Rather than steerage, the least-expensive fare was third (or sometimes fourth) class. Similar to steerage class, ships carried from 800 to 1,500 third-class passengers. Instead of open dormitories, these ships often had staterooms with anywhere from two to twelve berths. There were dedicated dining rooms, and passengers could walk on the promenade deck. Third-class passage on one of the newer ships was almost as comfortable as second class. When Mrs. Steinberg and her children sailed on the *Carpathia* in 1904, it was a new ship. Built in 1902, it had been sailing the Liverpool-to-Boston route for just over a year.[32]

Nonetheless, there were limited facilities for washing, even in the newer ships. Jacob Sadow's wife, Libby, and their six sons traveled on the Dominion Line's ship *Canada* from Liverpool to Boston in 1903. Sadow's niece, Sue, recalled that when her uncle Jacob arrived in Plymouth with his family, "the smell in our kitchen was overwhelming. They had all been on the boat for many days, traveling in steerage, and had probably slept in their clothes the whole time."[33]

Upon arrival in America, the immigrants had to go through several inspections, both legal and medical. Until 1890, passengers arriving in New York were processed at Castle Island. The increased rate of immigration over the 1880s proved too much for the antiquated facility, so a new inspection station, Ellis Island, opened in 1892. First- and second-class passengers were processed onboard the ship, as officials assumed that those able to afford more expensive passage were less likely to become a drain on their new country. Third-class travelers had to travel by ferry to Ellis Island. The health of the new arrivals was a major concern, so immigrants were examined for various diseases. The process could be harrowing. For instance, if the inspectors found the contagious eye disease trachoma, the immigrant was isolated and might even be sent back. Inspectors used a shoe buttonhook to flip the immigrant's eyelid back to check for the disease.

Arrival in Boston was less complicated. For one thing, there was no centrally located immigration station like Ellis Island for New York. At the beginning of the twentieth century, there were several places for steamships to dock. Cunard ships berthed at the Boston and Albany wharves, located in East Boston and run by the Boston and Albany railway line. White Star and Dominion line ships docked at the Hoosac wharves in Charlestown. Commonwealth Pier was not established as a landing place for transatlantic ships until circa 1915. Each line had an inspection station at the wharf where its ships landed. Once the immigrants passed through inspection, they could go to the adjacent train station to travel to their final destinations.[34]

A common myth is that the immigration inspectors at the port of arrival changed the immigrants' names to sound more American. For example, Mitchell Toabe recalled how his father's name, Mottel Toibe, was changed to Max Toabe when he arrived. Recently, historians have determined that immigration inspectors checked the records from the port of embarkation, dispelling the myth that names were changed upon arrival in America. The ship's manifest for the *Cephalonia*, which arrived in Boston from Liverpool on June 24, 1895, lists him as Moses Taub.

Arriving at the pier or railway station to pick up one's family must have been an emotional experience, particularly after years of separation. Max Toabe arrived in Boston in 1895 and was able to send for his wife and children four years later. The Toabes arrived on the *Catalonia* at the Boston and Albany wharves, where Max met his sons, his father and his sister, but not his wife. Sarah Berger Toabe had died—probably just before the journey from Liverpool, as she does not appear on the passenger list.

Births onboard ship were not uncommon. Morris Resnick left his wife, Celia, in London to set up a home in Plymouth in 1902. Celia, who was several months pregnant, arrived a month later onboard the *New England* at the

Shriber family, circa 1900. *Left to right*: Rebecca, Max and Gertrude. *Courtesy of the Klasky family.*

Copper pan brought by the Shriber family from Odessa around 1900. *Author photo.*

Hoosac wharves. According to granddaughter Rollene Waterman, "Part of my family lore is that my sainted grandmother Celia…lived alone and pregnant, making shirts in London's Petticoat Lane, with her tenement neighbors not believing she was a married woman. She told me that on the solo voyage to America, the ship nurse would follow her around and say, 'Frau Resnick, why not have the baby on the boat?'" Fortunately, daughter Hattie Rachel waited several weeks after the voyage to be born.[35]

What did immigrants bring on the journey? In addition to clothing and trunks, many brought religious items that represented their Jewish identity and traditions. The Shribers, who came from Odessa to Philadelphia, brought Shabbos candlesticks, as well as copper pots and a samovar for everyday use. The Brodys, who emigrated from Vilna to Boston, took with them a *siddur* (prayer book), which is still used by Congregation Beth Jacob for High Holy Days services. Everyday things were important to starting new lives as well. The Kabelskys brought feather pillows and *pierzyni*, or feather-stuffed blankets/mattresses.

COMING TO PLYMOUTH

It is not known what attracted the first Jews to Plymouth, but employment opportunities were a major factor. While Plymouth did have many industries, most of the early immigrants worked on their own as peddlers rather than

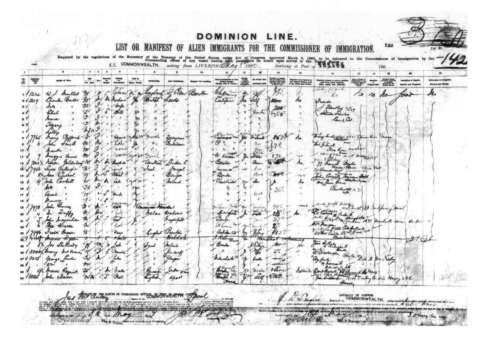

Passenger list of the SS *Commonwealth*, Liverpool to Boston, May 8, 1902. Morris Reznik (Resnick) is second from the bottom of the list. Column 16 shows that Morris was joining his uncle David Resnick in Plymouth. Column 9 indicates that his last residence was London.

in factories. Plymouth was of sufficient size to support shops and businesses, and many Jewish immigrants started as peddlers and worked their way from peddling to running their own stores. Moving to Plymouth may also have been a way for immigrants to escape the crowded tenements of Boston. Sue Sadow stated that many immigrants were met at the port in Boston by Jewish agents, who urged them to move to nearby towns instead of staying in the city. When her uncle Jacob's family arrived in Boston in 1906 from Liverpool, they were transferred to Plymouth, as none of the Boston relatives had room in their apartments.[36]

Ties of family and *mishpocha* (extended family) also led people to Plymouth. Brothers Louis and David Resnick, both from Krackenova (Kreckenava), were joined by nephews and nieces and were related by marriage to several families in town. Sarah Besbris Orentlicher, originally from Alayka, Ukraine, had been living in Plymouth for about fifteen years when her sister Rebecca (Rivka) Dezoretts and her family settled there. Soon after, their sister Elizabeth (Buni) Sklar and her family arrived for a short time before moving to Connecticut. Synagogue records show that a brother (probably Abraham) also lived in town for a while.[37]

Postcard, Plymouth Railroad Station, Park Street, Plymouth, Massachusetts, circa 1900. The New York, New Haven and Hartford Railroad ran from Boston's South Station to Plymouth, which was the end of the line. The Pyzanskis rode the train south from Boston to find a place to live "in the country" and chose Plymouth. *Collection of author.*

A shared village of origin was another reason that some people settled in Plymouth. Other immigrants came to Plymouth from Krackenova besides the Resnicks, including Abraham Frim and Ida Snyder Kabelsky. The Jewish population of the town was only 1,505 in 1897, so chances are the families knew each other. Rebecca Dezoretts's husband, Israel, came from Buki, near Kiev. After a few years in Plymouth, he sponsored a young man from his village, Joseph Cohen, to come to America and settle in town.[38]

One family moved to Plymouth for health reasons. Fannie Brody, who came from Vilna, married Max Pyzanski in Boston in the 1890s. When her health deteriorated due to bronchial infections, her doctor urged her to "move to the country." Asking around, Max's brother Moe was advised to take the train from Boston's South Station to find a suitable town. Moe took the train and rode it south to the end of the line—Plymouth. He found that there were other Jewish families and encouraged his brother Max and his family to settle there.[39]

The presence of Jews attracted other Jewish newcomers, and the community grew. By the early 1900s, there were enough Jewish families in town to form at least one *minyan.*

Chapter 3

Building a Congregation

FOUNDING A CONGREGATION

Even before there was a synagogue, Plymouth's Jews managed to observe the High Holy Days. Prior to 1909 or so, there was no rabbi or cantor, so the community invited religious leaders from Boston to lead Rosh Hashanah and Yom Kippur services. During the rest of the year, the community relied on local scholars to lead services and teach children Hebrew. Several men were learned and helped lead services. Jacob Steinberg, who lived in Plymouth by 1904, served as the *shochet* (person who slaughtered animals according to kosher laws) for many years.[40]

The first Hebrew teacher was most likely Michel Toabe, father of Max. Michel had escorted Max's family from Russia to Plymouth in late 1899, as Max's wife, Sarah, had died. Although he had intended to return to Russia, he decided to stay in Plymouth. He lived with his son's family and taught Hebrew until his death in 1906.

While Max Toabe was a rather strict man with regard to religion, his father, Michel, had a liberal interpretation of Jewish law. Max's sons Samuel and Kebe (from Akiva) were nine and six years old when they arrived in America in 1899 and had to adjust to going to school and playing with gentile children. Mitchell Toabe, their younger brother, recalled their stories about grandfather Michel. One day, the boys asked their father if they could go skating on the Sabbath. He automatically said no. Both carrying ice skates and cutting the ice with the skate blades might be

Michel Toabe, circa 1905, was Plymouth's first Hebrew teacher. *Courtesy of the Sherman family.*

considered work, which was forbidden on *Shabbat* (Sabbath). When they asked their grandfather, he said, "Let us consider the situation. If you should happen to go to services and have your skates with you…and you should go to a frozen pond that other people have skated on so no matter how much you skate, you aren't cutting the ice…that's not so bad."[41]

In another instance, the brothers asked if they could go to a ballgame in the next town, also on *Shabbat*. Traveling on the Sabbath was forbidden to traditional Jews. Again, it could be considered work. Grandfather Michel evaluated their request. While others might have automatically denied the boys permission to travel on the Sabbath, Michel carefully considered the definition of "the next town." "If you can see the roofs of one town from the other, without a break in houses, that's not traveling," he said.[42]

Without a space of their own to meet for High Holy Days, the community rented space in local public buildings, such as the Town House (now the 1749 Courthouse) in Town Square and the Red Men's Hall on Middle Street (above what became Arons furniture store). Using public buildings for

Town Square, Plymouth, Massachusetts, circa 1900. The wooden structure at the left is the 1749 Town House. Before the synagogue was built, members of Plymouth's Jewish community held holiday services in public halls. One of these was located on the second floor of the Town House. *Courtesy of Plimoth Plantation.*

Rosh Hashanah greeting card with a photograph of the Sherman family, 1908. Abram Sherman is standing, holding son Louis Sherman, while Sarah Toabe Sherman is seated in front. *Courtesy of the Sherman family.*

religious services was hardly new in Plymouth—in the 1850s, the Catholic community also used the Town House, prior to the construction of St. Peter's Church in 1874. Community members adapted the spaces to their religious requirements. "A dealer loaned the necessaries for setting up the altar with the ark with sliding doors where the Holy Scrolls were ensconced, complete with a velvet cover and gold fringe trimming, a sculpture of the ten commandments, and the eternal light…a cloth drapery extended the full width of the hall to divide the space" between men and women. The congregation's minutes mention a rental fee of six dollars, twice as much as the annual membership dues once the congregation was established.[43]

Weekly services were conducted in members' homes. Sarah Toabe Sherman kept the Torah scrolls at her home during the week. Sarah, who was the sister of Max Toabe, came over with Max's children and Michel Toabe in 1899. In 1905, Sarah married Abram Sherman, who worked as a junk dealer. They set up housekeeping at 106 Sandwich Street, just south of the Town Brook and a ten-minute walk from downtown Plymouth.[44]

It was not unusual for small congregations in the early years of the century to meet in members' homes or storefronts. Since people preferred worshipping with others from their region of origin, a city might have several small congregations. The city of New Bedford, for instance, had two *landsleit* groups (from same place of origin). Poles and Lithuanians generally met separately from Russians. As small communities of recent immigrants, members could not afford to pay a full-time rabbi or maintain a synagogue.[45]

Even before a congregation was established in Plymouth, there was a split. Residents divided into two *minyans*, based on where they came from. By the time there were twenty families, the community had split into the Litvak group and the Russian group. "They used to fight like hell. Because each had their own enunciation, each read the Hebrew differently…they used to come to actual fistfights."[46]

In 1909, the community established a single body, the Jacob Beis Society, that soon comprised more than forty families. The incorporation papers, dated March 15, 1909, list seven men: Kasiel Simon Bass, Joseph Berg, Julius Cohen, Louis Goldstein, Abraham Kaplow, Bernard Seldeen and Max Shriber. David Resnick was the first president, assisted by Jacob Steinberg as treasurer and Samuel Snyder as secretary. Officers of the congregation met twice monthly in Rabbi Abraham Nathanson's house on High Street.

Dues were modest—only twenty-five cents a month and two dollars for new members. Those wanting to join had to be nominated by a member and voted on by the congregation. Non-members were charged for *yahrzeits*

Rabbi Abraham Nathanson's house at 55–57 High Street, 1960. Before the synagogue was built, Plymouth's Jewish community met in many places, including Rabbi Nathanson's home. Abraham's wife, Miriam, bought the property from Bessie Markus in 1908. The house is no longer standing. *Courtesy of the Plymouth Redevelopment Authority.*

(observance of the anniversary of a loved one's death). Each August, the congregation voted to pay Rabbi Nathanson to serve as *Baal Mussof* (*Musaf*), or leader of special holy day prayers, for High Holy Days services, with a salary of forty to sixty dollars. *Shokhet* Jacob Steinberg served as *Baal Shakris* (*Shacharit*), or leader of the daily morning service, for twenty-five dollars. An additional fee was paid to a member to blow the *shofar* (ram's horn).[47]

Building a Synagogue

It took a year to find a suitable site on which to build a synagogue. The congregation needed to find an affordable lot in the area where the majority of Plymouth's Jewish community lived. Travel other than walking could be considered work, and since work and travel were forbidden on the Sabbath, the synagogue needed to be close enough to people's homes that they could walk. In January 1910, the congregation purchased a lot at the corner of Pleasant and Sandwich Streets, just south of Town Square, for $1,900. The neighborhood was one of the oldest in Plymouth—a house and tavern had stood a few yards east of the lot in the seventeenth century. The lot, with a small house, had been owned by the Harlow family for generations.[48]

Several people can be credited with the purchase of the land. In a heated discussion with a competitor (one of the Sadows), peddler Joseph Berg offered to buy the land. Berg had long been interested in real estate and had bought land in North Plymouth and built at least two storefront apartments on Court Street. In exchange for arranging the purchase of the land, Berg received the seat in front of the *bimah* (podium for reading the Torah scrolls). Sue Sadow remembered a slightly different story. Her uncle Jacob, a very Orthodox Jew, disapproved of using the town hall for religious services. He dreamed of a synagogue where people could worship and boys could study for their *bar mitzvahs*. Jacob, a peddler, faithfully solicited contributions from his customers, both Jewish and gentile. He saved the contributions to help purchase the plot.[49]

At a special meeting, the congregation authorized the officers to secure a mortgage of $1,500 from local businessman Charles B. Stoddard, which was discharged a few months later when they secured other funding. In December 1913, soon after the synagogue was completed, the congregation secured two mortgages: one for up to $4,000 with the Plymouth Five Cents Savings Bank and one with David Resnick and Joseph Berg for $2,000.[50]

Members met every two weeks to manage progress on the building. Fundraising events, including a Purim ball, helped garner enough money to start building. To raise additional money, members bid on seats, priced according to their proximity to the ark or *bimah*. It was typical of Orthodox synagogues in the early twentieth century that men had specific seats on the main floor and women received seats in the gallery above that corresponded to their husbands' places. Members also bid on who would light the eternal flame when the synagogue opened. Each Sunday, two members traveled to visit Jews in nearby cities, including New Bedford, Quincy, Malden and Lawrence, to solicit money for the construction of the synagogue. The congregation sold the house on the east part of the lot to the Dezoretts family, which also helped raise necessary funds.[51]

In 1912, the congregation laid the cornerstone for the synagogue, on the west side of the small lot. The wooden building was designed by an engineer from the Plymouth Cordage Company and built by contractor John Miller of Boston. The building somewhat reflected the Gothic Revival style, with an imposing gable facing Pleasant Street. A pair of arched windows flanked the wide arched door, with a Star of David in the round colored-glass window above. Designed in the traditional manner inside, the *bimah* was located in the center surrounded by pews, with a gallery for women and girls upstairs and a *mikvah* (ritual bath) in the basement. While traditional in function, the building had modern features, including a cement foundation, steam heat and electricity and gas for lighting. Although the building was not finished, the High Holy Days were celebrated in there in the fall of 1912, with services led by Rabbis Nathanson and Steinberg.[52]

Façade of Congregation Beth Jacob's synagogue, 1960. The synagogue was built in 1912–13 and dedicated in December 1913. *Courtesy of the Plymouth Redevelopment Authority.*

The dedication of Congregation Beth Jacob's synagogue, December 28, 1913. The synagogue is on the right, with Market Street in the background. *Courtesy of Congregation Beth Jacob.*

Construction was completed late in 1913, and the dedication of the synagogue in December was a memorable occasion for the small congregation that had worked for so many years to achieve its goal—its own Jewish house of worship in its new hometown. Rose Sherman Geller, whose parents, aunts and uncles were among the founders present at the dedication, wrote how the scene looked that day:

> *The whole congregation stands out on the street eagerly awaiting the arrival of horse-drawn carriages—men in their derby hats and topcoats, women in the most elegant finery and large feathered hats, the children in their polished high-buttoned shoes. A carriage, drawn by two white horses, pulls up in front of the Synagogue, follow[ed] by a second carriage with a team of black horses. Two men dressed in top hats, morning coats and striped pants descend from the first carriage, tenderly carrying two precious Torahs.[53]*

The dedication of the synagogue attracted the attention of the local newspaper. The reporter described the interior:

The ceiling is done in three shades of blue…and the walls are in buff tints, while the ornamentation is derived from the Egyptian. The dado is of conventionalized papyrus leaves, while the frieze is of old Egyptian ornament, representing the papyrus and the waves of the Nile…Directly above the tabernacle are the spread wings representing speed and strength and still higher are vases of lotus flowers with sacred palms. The ornamentation is in tints of sienna and pale green. The star of David in the eastern window with its white ground, is repeated in the centre pieces of the ceiling and in the chandelier…The decoration is the work of C.H. Badger & Son.[54]

Religious leaders from both Plymouth and Boston attended the dedication. "The Jews are the first Pilgrims in history…they crossed the Euphrates river to escape from tyranny and oppression," said Reverend Dr. P. Israeli of Boston. Reverend C.F. Andrews of the First Universalist Society of Plymouth commented, "The Christian church was an outgrowth of Judaism; that the world's progress was due to the Jewish race." Reverend Arthur B. Whitney of the First Church in Plymouth extended his congratulations: "The Pilgrims' gift of a free and open faith is brought to you."[55]

The following rabbis and scholars led the congregation through 1940: Michel Toabe (1895–1906), Abraham Nathanson (until his death in 1926), Jacob Steinberg (circa 1900 until his death in 1926), Reverend Samuel Krinsky (mid-1910s), Rabbi Lippins (left in 1922), Rabbi Baras (started in 1922), Rabbi Abraham Goldbergh (early 1930s) and Rabbi Samuel Friedman (1936–41).[56]

OBSERVING JUDAISM

Plymouth's Jewish community came together from several different traditions. Like the vast majority of Jews who arrived in America around the turn of the century, almost all were Orthodox. Joseph Berg was extremely *frum* (devout), and his descendants remembered hearing how he would not allow his daughters to brush their hair on Shabbat, as that could be considered a type of work. Jacob Sadow was very observant, according to his niece Sue Sadow: "Every morning my uncle Jacob rose very early and said all the prayers…It was understood that no one could speak to him to interrupt him while he was praying." Many people refused to talk on the telephone on Shabbat, as the operator had to work. Women cooked their Saturday meals the day before so they did not have to work on the Sabbath.[57]

One way to get around the strict laws forbidding many types of work on the Sabbath was to have a non-Jewish person, who was not observing the holy day, perform the task. One of the many kinds of work forbidden on Shabbat is lighting a fire. Many Jewish families and congregations hired a *goy* (non-Jew) to turn on the lights and/or heat. At least one family used a "Shabbos Goy" to light their stove.[58]

The Dezoretts family, as well as many others, were *shomer Shabbat*, or strictly observant of the Sabbath laws. That meant that not only did a person not work on Saturday, but he or she also had to leave work before sundown on Friday night, when the Sabbath began. This schedule posed a problem for factory workers with set shifts, which usually included Saturday work. Because of this challenge, many Jewish immigrants to Plymouth worked for themselves as peddlers or merchants. One local industry provided some flexibility. Israel Dezoretts and his son Solomon worked for the Plymouth Stove Foundry on Water Street. As the foundry was Jewish-owned at the time, the job allowed the Dezorettses and other Jewish workers to be observant and not work on the Sabbath.[59]

Many families, including the Dezorettses, kept strictly kosher. They purchased kosher meat from Boston and maintained two sets of dishes in their kitchen, one for *milchik* (dairy) and the other for *fleishik* (meat) food. Many even had additional sets of dishes for Passover. Neighbor Nancy Kabelsky Cutler, who lived across the street from Mrs. Dezoretts, used to deliver Mr. Dezoretts's lunch to him at the foundry; she'd hand it in through the window where he worked.[60]

The late Mitchell Toabe referred to Simon Orentlicher as Chassidic and remembered that he danced at services. Chassidism, a mystical movement of Judaism founded by the Rabbi Israel Baal Shem Tov in the mid-eighteenth century, emphasized joy and included much singing and dancing. Simon's granddaughter did not recall his being Chassidic, but he did come from Volhynia guberniya, an area of the Ukraine with Chassidic traditions.[61]

Other members of the community were less observant, beginning to assimilate into American society. Sue Sadow recalled that her father was "always too busy to say all the prayers that were expected of the Orthodox Jew." He kept his head covered with a hat, except when in his store or while visiting gentiles. Some businessmen even began keeping their shops open on Saturdays. A few members of the community, including Meyer Shwom, did not participate in services for political reasons, although he made sure his children learned Hebrew.[62]

Simon and Sarah Orentlicher with two of their sons, Jack and Benjamin, circa 1900. *Courtesy of Leila Wolfe.*

Like many Orthodox synagogues in the early twentieth century, services must have been somewhat chaotic. On the main floor, men and boys prayed, frequently using different tunes and pronunciation of Hebrew, based on where they came from. Above in the gallery sat women and girls. Fannie Steinberg occupied the center seat. Rose Sherman Geller recalled that Mrs. Steinberg was very good at Hebrew, and women used to sit next to her to better follow the service. Rose remembered sitting in the gallery as a girl, giggling with her young friends and garnering many angry looks from the men praying below. Her father would murmur, "*Lo zein shah*" ("Be quiet!") to silence the girls in the balcony above.[63]

Women continued to sit in the gallery into the 1940s. Mel Klasky recalled escorting his grandmother, Rebecca Shriber, to synagogue every Saturday morning. She sat upstairs, on the right side. Ina Zall Cutler remembered sitting downstairs for Friday night Shabbat services as a girl in the late 1930s, but women still used the gallery for other holy days. The *mikvah* appears to have gone out of use by that time.[64]

Tzedakah (charity), as well as prayer, was an important part of religious life. Sue Sadow's family kept *pushkes* (boxes or cans to collect coins) fastened to the counter of their kitchen, one for each of several charities. Both adults and children contributed to the boxes. Sadow recalled that the "collectors

Sabbath candlesticks brought by the Shriber family from Odessa around 1900. *Author photo.*

came several times a year. They were religious Jewish men, dressed in long black coats and round black hats trimmed with fur…They drank tea in glasses that Mama offered them."[65]

While women did not have significant roles in the operation of the synagogue, they were very active in fundraising. Sarah Toabe Sherman was one of the founders of the Beth Jacob Ladies' Aid Society, a forerunner to the Sisterhood. Mrs. Steinberg led the group, which met in her kitchen next door to the synagogue. Members paid dues of ten cents a month. The society was a *gemillas chesed*, or charitable organization, and raised money for various projects, like buying mantles or covers for the Torah scrolls. One of its purposes was to help local Jewish businessmen with small loans. These loans helped members of the community as they struggled to make a living in their new environment.[66]

Chapter 4

Making a Living

Between its port, industries and transportation connections, turn-of-the-century Plymouth had a lot to offer newcomers. The largest town in Massachusetts in terms of land mass, Plymouth measures almost twenty miles from north to south. By 1910, more than twelve thousand people lived there, most clustered around downtown and North Plymouth. Small farms were scattered outside the heavily populated areas. While not a deep-water port like Boston, Plymouth's small harbor boasted thirteen wharfs that landed boats laden with anything from hemp and coal to tourists visiting Plymouth Rock. With Plymouth's wharfs, railroad links to Boston and Middleboro and electric streetcar link to Brockton, merchants could receive and ship goods. Industries like textile mills, ropeworks and iron foundries lined the town's waterways, providing employment for thousands. It was not difficult for an immigrant, male or female, to find a job in one of the town's many factories. Many who came to Plymouth, particularly those from Italy and Portugal, worked for industries like the Plymouth Cordage Company or one of the many woolen mills. The concentrated population created opportunities for merchants and tradesmen to establish businesses.

While sons and daughters of Jewish immigrants often worked in the mills, most of the first generation of Jewish immigrants tended to work for themselves. Large towns like Plymouth had substantial enough populations to support peddlers, shopkeepers and tradesmen. Many Jewish immigrants started as peddlers and subsequently opened stores of their own. Peddling allowed immigrants with limited skills in the English language to work when and where they wanted to.

Junk Dealers

Many newcomers started as junk dealers—including David Resnick, Max Toabe, Morris B. Resnick, his brother Simon Resnick, Harry Frim, David Karnofsky, Esser Milner and Abram Sherman. All they needed was a horse and wagon. According to Sue Sadow, "They turned to rag picking and became rag peddlers as it required only a few words in English. As rag peddlers, they could be independent. With the help of their wives and children, they could sort out items from the day's collection, which they could sell for cash." Some collected scrap metal or glass as well. Many new peddlers were not aware that they had to pay a two-dollar license tax to the town and got in trouble. Town officials appealed to established Jewish merchants like Max Sadow, who spoke good English, to help translate.[67]

One of the best-known characters in twentieth-century Plymouth was junk dealer Harry Frim, who lived on Union Street near the yacht club. He traveled all over town with his horse and wagon, collecting rags, bottles and scrap metal. Many older residents recall hearing him call out "Ju-unk!" to announce his presence. Frim was known for his prodigious strength. Joe Busi, interviewed in his nineties, recalled that local kids used to ask Frim to lift his horse for them. By putting his back under the horse and lifting, he could raise the horse completely off the ground.[68]

The darndest stunt I ever saw him pull was moving a stove. A fellow was remodeling his house and he had one of those big old black iron stoves with the hood on the top. He told Harry that he could have the stove if he could take it down the stairs. Harry Frim went upstairs and disassembled the stove and got it ready to take down. He called down that he was ready and needed some help…After a while Harry tapped at the window and said, "Never mind." He had that kitchen stove on his back complete. He'd taken all the loose things and thrown them in the oven…It must have weighed five or six hundred pounds.[69]

While some junk dealers collected rags, others specialized in old furniture. Mayer Markus sold secondhand furniture (as well as coal) near Town Square as early as 1911. For a time, Kasiel Simon Bass, who also owned a variety store, sold secondhand furniture. Max Shriber is listed as an umbrella repairman in early street directories but had expanded to used furniture by 1919. Around that time, his daughter Gertrude married Hyman Klasky, a cabinetmaker who grew up in Boston's West End, a

Abram Sherman at his furniture store at 301 Court Street, Plymouth, Massachusetts, circa 1925. *Courtesy of the Sherman family.*

neighborhood of Jewish immigrants. By 1921, the two men specialized in antiques. Max's business continued through three generations—Klasky took over the business after Shriber's death in 1924, and his son Melvin ran an antique store on Union Street through the early 2000s.

Abram Sherman ran a junk business with a shop in the Emond Building on Main Street. He specialized in furniture, and gradually his business grew to include hardware and paint. Around 1923, he expanded his business to North Plymouth, and by the end of the 1920s, he was successful enough to build a three-story storefront at 310 Court Street. Even after his death in 1930, his family continued to operate two stores. The North Plymouth location became an Ethan Allen store and remained in business into the 1990s.

Dealing in junk could be a lucrative endeavor. David Resnick, who arrived in New York in 1889, first appears in the Plymouth street directory in 1896. He made his living as a junk dealer, starting small but becoming significant. Resnick took advantage of Plymouth's many industries, buying their cast-off material. Mitchell Toabe recalled that he had an arrangement with the Plymouth Cordage Company for its scrap. He may also have been involved with the Plymouth Stove Foundry.[70]

From Peddlers to Merchants

While some collected items to recycle, others sold goods, either as peddlers or as shopkeepers. Shopkeepers generally started as peddlers until they could afford stores of their own. Some peddlers were lucky enough to have horses and wagons so they could travel to nearby towns. Others walked the streets with packs on their backs. Sue Sadow remembered that her uncle Jacob walked the streets carrying his stock. He was "all bent over under his heavy load that reached from his shoulders to his ankles."[71]

Max Toabe peddled pots and pans until, around 1907, he was approached by Luigi Cortelli (L. Knife), who owned several buildings in North Plymouth. "Why don't you sell your pots and pans in one of my empty stores?" Cortelli proposed. Max protested that he didn't have enough money to pay rent. "Don't worry," Cortelli replied. "You can pay me rent when you earn enough money." One day a man at the railroad station showed Max a load of damaged goods. "Why don't you take these," he suggested, "and have your family fix them to sell in your

Peddler Joseph Berg with his horse and wagon in downtown Kingston, Massachusetts, 1890. *Courtesy of Joan M. Tieman.*

JOSEPH BERG.

DEALER IN

Dry Goods, Clothing,

Boots, Shoes and Rubbers. Jewelry, etc.

289 COURT ST., NORTH PLYMOUTH.

Plymouth street directory advertisement for Joseph Berg's dry goods business, 1896.

store?" Thus began Toabe's Hardware, a chain of stores on the South Shore that lasted for several decades.[72]

Shopkeeping did not preclude peddling. Often wives would mind the store while their husbands took a horse and wagon and peddled in nearby towns too small to support their own stores. Joseph Berg is listed in 1896 as having a dry goods store at 289 Court Street in North Plymouth. A photograph shows him with his horse and wagon near the railroad tracks in Kingston, the next town to the north. Max Sadow had a clothing store, first on Russell Street and then near the Town Square. Daughter Sue Sadow remembered that it had a blue flashing electric sign—the first in town—and people used to walk by just to look at it. A couple days a week, his wife, Celia, would watch the store while he took a horse and wagon to smaller towns to peddle men's and boys' clothing.[73]

Another peddler, a Mr. Rosen, was a minor participant in one of the Boston area's most infamous events of the early twentieth century. In 1920, Bartolomeo Vanzetti, an Italian immigrant and anarchist who lived in North Plymouth, was accused of robbing an armored car in South Braintree, along with fellow anarchist Nicola Sacco. Two people were killed during the robbery, and the men were charged with murder. While many residents and workers from North Plymouth swore that they had seen Vanzetti selling fish at the time he was supposed to have been committing the robbery, prosecutors tore apart the testimony of the immigrant witnesses, many of whom could not speak English. Sacco and Vanzetti were convicted of the crime and executed in 1927.

Years later, folk musician and poet Woody Guthrie was commissioned to write *The Ballads of Sacco and Vanzetti*. In a song called "Suassos Lane" (Suosso Lane), Guthrie mentions a peddler named Rosen:

> *Goodbye, my comrades,*
> *Goodbye, my north Plymouth,*
> *Goodbye to the Boston harbor,*
> *Goodbye, Suassos Lane.*
> *Suassos Lane is just an alley*
> *Up here in old north Plymouth.*
> *You saw my fish cart*
> *Roll here in Suassos Lane…*
>
> *My name is Joseph Rosen,*
> *I am a woolen peddler,*
> *I sold Vanzetti a roll of cloth,*
> *That day in Suassos Lane.*
>
> *I'm Mrs. Alphonsine Brini,*
> *Mr. Rosen and Bart Vanzetti*
> *Showed me the cloth with big hole in it.*
> *One block from Suassos Lane.*[74]

Fannie Pyzanski's house at 58 High Street, Plymouth, Massachusetts, 1960. Fannie lived in part of the home with her children and rented the rest to tenants. She owned the house from 1911 until 1927. *Courtesy of the Plymouth Redevelopment Authority.*

An Aaron Rosen appears in the 1920 census for Plymouth living with his wife, Flora Smith Rosen, and her family on South Street. While Aaron is listed as a salesman in a men's clothing store rather than as a peddler, sometimes people who worked in shops also peddled.

Not all peddlers were men. A few years after the Pyzanskis moved to Plymouth for Fannie's health, Max died, leaving her with a son and daughter to support. A well-off cousin in Boston urged her to move back to the city, but Fannie was determined to stand on her own. "As long as I have two hands," she said, "I will take care of my children." Fannie's granddaughter Muriel Swartz recalled that her grandmother sold sewing goods door-to-door to her neighbors and friends to support her family. Longtime *Old Colony Memorial* reporter Maggie Mills remembered that Mrs. Pyzanski sold secondhand children's clothes, in particular a pair of cashmere infant booties that "caressed a baby's foot." Fannie continued peddling until she was well into her seventies—"visiting her old acquaintances, more than business."[75]

Lillian Snyder, Lilyan Kabelsky and Bessie Resnick at Plymouth beach, 1925.
Courtesy of Nancy Kabelsky Cutler.

Jewish merchants operated many of Plymouth's clothing and shoe stores. Samuel Levine opened Puritan Clothing in downtown Plymouth circa 1909. Louis Rubenstein started as an employee of Samuel Medved's shop, Old Colony Clothing, and eventually became proprietor of Standish Clothing. Max Sadow's son Phil continued in the family clothing business, opening Sadow's Women's Shop at 38 Court Street near the Courthouse in the early 1920s. The Student brothers, Joseph and Hyman, operated a shoe store at 47 Main Street. In North Plymouth, Meyer Shwom and his brother Ellis ran a store at 305 Court Street. Women also worked in clothing stores, and working in a shop was considered a good job. Several daughters of Jewish immigrants chose this occupation, including Lilyan Kabelsky. Her sister Nancy recalled that Lilyan always looked very fashionable.[76]

Jews in neighboring communities also ran clothing stores. Benjamin Feinberg and his family operated a clothing store on Ocean Street in Marshfield as early as 1910, the Shiffs opened a store in Duxbury in 1918 and the Sadows' brother Joseph sold clothing in Wareham. Often these families were the only Jews in town. The occurrence of a single Jewish family operating a dry goods store in a gentile community was common throughout America, as seen in Stella Suberman's book *The Jew Store*, about a Jewish family who owned a store in a small Tennessee town. In New England as well, many retailers were Jewish, particularly in smaller communities like Laconia, New Hampshire, and Great Barrington, Massachusetts.[77]

Many stores expanded to nearby towns. Fannie Pyzanski's son Abraham left school at age sixteen to pursue a retail career. According to family stories, he could do the math problems faster than the teacher. Unbeknownst to his mother, he had started in sales while still in school, helping peddler Harry Frim sell potatoes. He moved to Roxbury to live with relatives in a crowded apartment, with three or four people sharing a bed, and soon found work in a shoe store. One day Abe Pyzanski met Samuel Levine in Boston. Levine ran Puritan Clothing in Plymouth and was looking for someone to staff a new shoe department that he was adding to his store. Pyzanski returned to Plymouth to work at Puritan Clothing.[78]

When Levine died in 1919, Abe and a colleague from the store, Achille Maccaferri, purchased the store, with the help of a loan from his mother, Fannie. Around this time, the entire family changed their name to Penn. The business prospered, and they soon opened branches in Rockland, Chatham and Hyannis. In the early 1950s, the Penns and Maccaferris divided the business. Maccaferri chose the Plymouth store, which closed circa 1990, while the Penns took the Hyannis store, still in existence in 2012. Abe

Abraham and Fannie Pyzanski, circa 1910. The family changed their last name to Penn in the early 1920s. *Courtesy of Milton Penn.*

Penn was admired for his business acumen. In spite of the fact that he'd never graduated high school, his classmates honored him with the "most successful" award at their fiftieth reunion.[79]

Other Jewish merchants ran variety stores, which sold merchandise ranging from hardware to Pilgrim souvenir china. Galician immigrant Kasiel Simon Bass opened a variety store on Market Street in Town Square around 1900. Two souvenir porcelain dishes with Pilgrim scenes, made in Austria or Germany, descended in the family of a congregant. On the bottom they are marked "Imported for K.S. Bass." Julius Cohen ran a variety store on Main Street in the early 1900s. Eventually, he purchased several adjacent buildings on Market Street and opened Cohen's Store, which sold both new and used furniture, along with small household items, rugs, linoleum and work clothes. His son Harris and his wife, Rose Skulsky Cohen, ran the store through the mid-1960s. The large sign with the Cohen name attracted the attention of Jews who were visiting Plymouth.[80]

Every immigrant group in Plymouth had grocers, and the Jews were no exception. By 1903, Louis and Ida Resnick had established a grocery store

Cohen's Store, Market Street, Plymouth, Massachusetts, 1960. Julius Cohen opened a store at this location circa 1925 that sold a variety of new and used household items. *Courtesy of Plymouth Redevelopment Authority.*

at their residence at 92 South Street, a frame house that is still standing today. Eventually, they opened a small store across the street where they sold candy, tobacco and magazines. On visits in the 1930s, grandson Bernard Resnick remembered watching his grandfather sitting in his store reading *Argosy* magazine. Bessie (Beile) Skulsky ran a small grocery store connected to the family home at 108 Sandwich Street.[81]

Sometimes a businessman who started small became very successful. Joseph Cohen, who came to America around 1908, started working at the Plymouth Cordage Company but decided it was not for him. He decided to open a wholesale candy business and rented a horse and wagon to deliver candy to small shops in towns from Cape Cod north to Kingston. Nephew Morris Bloom remembered asking how he was able to make a living from his business. Cohen replied that even after deducting the price of the horse and wagon, he earned five dollars per week, almost twice what the average worker at the Cordage Company made.[82]

Shops on the east side of Market Street, circa 1960. People's Market is at the left of the photo. Joseph Cohen and Julius Sepet ran the market until Cohen's death in 1945. Cohen's nephew, Morris Bloom, and Jack Minsky operated the store from 1945 until the mid-1960s, when the store was demolished as part of an urban renewal project. *Courtesy of Plymouth Redevelopment Authority.*

Shortly before World War I, Joseph opened a grocery store at 41 Summer Street, an apartment building built by another Jewish family, the Markuses. His draft registration lists him as a self-employed grocer. After the war, Joseph joined forces with Julius Sepet, a meat cutter, to open several grocery stores. Sepet, who boarded with the Steinbergs, had worked for several years at the Plymouth Cordage Company. It is possible that he learned butchering from Steinberg, who served as the local *shochet*.

In 1920, Cohen married Sylvia Rubinfein, and the couple moved into a house down the street that he had bought a couple of years earlier. They ran a grocery store, National D. Market, which catered to the local Jewish population. Before long they operated three other stores in the Plymouth area: People's Market on Market Street; Pioneer Market on Main Street Extension, across from the post office; and a store at the Federal Cranberry Bog in Carver for Cape Verdean cranberry workers. On Friday nights, the

S. SHOMAN
Merchant Tailor
Ladies' and Gent's Garments made in up-to-date Style and Finish
Garments Cleaned and Pressed

Plymouth street directory advertisement for Samuel Shoman's tailoring business, circa 1905.

men came in from the cranberry bogs to People's Market to shop and talk about their families back home in Cape Verde. Daughter Gladys remembered roasting potatoes and chestnuts for the men.[83]

Many Jewish immigrants were involved in the clothing trade, not just as peddlers and merchants but also as tradesmen. Tailoring was a very common occupation in Russia, and there were at least ten tailors in Plymouth's Jewish community. Simon Orentlicher is listed as a tailor in the street directory as early as 1893, but in 1905, he is listed as a clothier, with a business near Town Square on Sandwich Street near the synagogue. By 1913, he specialized in woolens and worsteds (several of Plymouth's textile mills produced woolens). Samuel Shoman and his son-in-law, Nathan Goldsmith, operated a tailoring business on Sandwich Street. His family recalled that they had a successful business doing alterations and custom work. Benjamin Dretler and Aldi Greenspoon had a tailoring business on Main Street for many years. Zitter and Maged had a shop in the Moore Building, while Abraham Kaplow, William Lewis and the Koblantz brothers worked in the Emond Building just south of Town Square. A few women, like Sarah Resnick, worked as dressmakers.

Several men worked as cobblers, including Louis Goldstein, Hyman Miller, Harry Gould and Abraham Aronovitch. Both Goldstein and Miller had shops downtown. Isadore Albert and his son Mannis had a small upholstery business on Main Street. There were even two Jewish photographers, Abraham Hurwitz and Samuel Rice. When Louis and Ida Resnick decided to have a family portrait taken, they went to Hurwitz, a fellow congregant.

Cigar making was a common profession for Jews in Boston, and Plymouth had some cigar makers as well. David Seldeen, Bernard Rappoport and Harry Glassman worked in the tobacco trade. As early as 1915, Glassman had a shop at the corner of Sandwich and Water Streets. Milton Penn recalled that "tobacco leaves hung in his attic and his house always had the pervading odor of tobacco." Mel Klasky used to help Mr. Glassman by blowing open the cellophane wrappers.[84]

OTHER TRADES

Other professions involved property and livestock. While Jews in Russia faced restrictions in purchasing agricultural land, many had lived and worked in the country. Outside of industrial towns, the South Shore of Boston was still rural, and cattle trading provided another business opportunity. Many families who lived outside of town kept a cow to provide milk, even after World War II. Cattle dealing was a common profession among Jewish immigrants in small-town New England—it allowed them to combine business and farming.[85]

Several members of the Jewish community, particularly the Resnicks and Skulskys, operated cattle businesses. Both Morris B. Resnick and his brother Simon were cattle dealers as early as the 1910s. Morris and his sons, William and Alton, used to travel by horse and wagon (later truck) between Cape Cod and Brockton to buy and sell cows. Much of the Cape was still rural, and urban Brockton had fairgrounds where animals were sold. By 1936, Morris had a farm in Kingston on Basler's Lane to keep the cattle, near his brother Simon's farm. Simon's son, another Morris, also

Truck, M.B. Resnick & Sons, Cattle Dealers, Plymouth, Massachusetts, circa 1940. *Courtesy of the Resnick family.*

Cattle dealer Morris B. Resnick with horse, circa 1935. *Courtesy of the Resnick family.*

kept a farm in Kingston, on Wapping Road (Route 106). In the 1930s, Barnet Skulsky purchased a farm in Manomet and became a cattle dealer, along with his sons George and Louis. Veterinarian Ray Russo remembered driving through the Pine Hills and seeing the Skulskys' red barn, where the entrance to Pilgrim Nuclear Plant is today.[86]

A couple of businessmen and women supplemented their incomes by buying and selling real estate. Around 1910, Mayer Markus and his wife, Bessie, began buying old houses or vacant lots in the center of town and building apartment houses. Considering that many Jewish immigrants were just starting out, centrally located apartments near the synagogue were welcome. Many Jewish families, including the Kabelskys, lived in the apartment building at 41 Summer Street built by the Markuses. They also built the Dezoretts house at 52 Summer Street, near Spring Lane.

Julius Cohen and his family were extremely active in real estate. In the early years of the century, Cohen purchased the old Central House Hotel on Main Street near North Street. He converted it to small apartments and renamed the building Shirley Inn due to its proximity to Shirley Square. Julius and his sons and daughters began buying and selling dozens of old houses in central Plymouth and rented them as tenements.

Shirley Square, looking north along Main Street, Plymouth, Massachusetts, circa 1900. The Central House hotel is on the left. Julius Cohen purchased the building and renamed it the Shirley Inn. *Courtesy of Plimoth Plantation.*

Reporter and longtime Plymouth resident Maggie Mills grew up in two of Cohen's apartments. Betty Covell Sander recalled that Cohen always painted his buildings yellow. Julius's son Harris continued the family tradition of real estate into the 1960s, supplying low-cost apartments to Plymoutheans, both Jewish and gentile.[87]

Factory Work

While most Jewish immigrants to Plymouth were self-employed, others took advantage of the many opportunities for factory work. While a self-employed trader like Joseph Cohen could make a better living than a Cordage Company worker, working in a mill was steadier and more reliable than working for one's self. A half dozen Jewish men worked for the Cordage Company at some point in their lives, including Frank Kabelsky, Louis Smith, Eli Meisel and Harry Frim. In addition to the Plymouth Cordage Company, one of the world's largest rope factories, Plymouth was home to several woolen mills. John Padlusky was a wool dyer. Several daughters of immigrants worked as seamstresses, speckers and winders.

At least eight men, fathers and sons, worked for one specific factory: the Plymouth Stove Foundry on Water Street at the harbor. Established in the mid-nineteenth century, the foundry made a variety of cast-iron goods, including a stove with a molded scene of the Pilgrims landing. By 1906, the foundry had fallen on hard times and was sold to out-of-state investors. The new owners included Adolph, Nettie and Lassar Grinberg of New York and Bernard Feldman. The Grinbergs were businessmen who had come from Bucharest, Romania, in the 1880s. Feldman, who had emigrated from Galatz, Romania, in 1902, moved to Plymouth with his family to become the foundry manager.[88]

The foundry offered a variety of jobs for both unskilled laborers and skilled metal workers. Several Jewish men worked as molders, including Israel Dezoretts, Nathaniel Udis and Louis Smith. Molders made forms for casting out of sand and other materials. Working in the foundry could be physically demanding, and Israel's granddaughter, Eunice, recalled

Plymouth Foundry, Water Street, Plymouth, Massachusetts, circa 1900. Several men among Plymouth's Jewish community worked at the foundry. *Courtesy of Donna D. Curtin.*

hearing that he was not a strong man, so his son Solomon helped him. Every morning before school, Sol went to the foundry to get the fires going to save his father the difficult toil. Solomon became a core maker, fabricating complex hollow molds. Because the foundry was Jewish-owned, it offered some flexibility for Jewish workers who were observant.[89]

Whether it was peddling, shopkeeping or factory work, making a living was an all-encompassing part of life, as immigrant parents strove to give their children more opportunities than they had.

Chapter 5

The Importance of Family

Family was the center of Jewish life in Europe, and the immigrants brought this cherished value with them as they began their new lives. Even when family bonds were torn apart by the immigration process, people strove to restore them as quickly as possible. Those who had lost a spouse went to a *shadchan* (matchmaker) to find a new mate. Husbands and wives who had lived apart for many years learned to live together again, and many added American-born children to their existing families. Over time, tension developed between parents who had grown up in Eastern Europe and their American-born children.

MARRIAGE

Perhaps the first Jewish marriage celebrated in Plymouth was between Max Toabe and Ida Schachter on July 26, 1899. It is not known who officiated, as there was no rabbi in town. Max had come to America from Russia on his own in the early 1890s, leaving his family behind to establish a new home for them. His wife, Sarah Berger Toabe, and two sons left Russia a few years later, accompanied by Max's sister Sarah and their father, Michel. When Max went to Boston to meet them, he discovered that his wife, Sarah, had died en route. Max had a difficult time making a living and taking care of two small boys, so he went to a *shadchan* and found a new wife, Ida. The couple went on to have six children of their own. Back in Russia, marriages were usually arranged; Joseph Berg met his wife, Ida Geneva, on their wedding day.[90]

Marrying again after the death of a spouse was not uncommon. David Resnick lost his wife, Sarah Lipsitz, in 1902 from consumption. Having two young sons to raise, he married Jennie Miller the next year in Plymouth. Mayer Markus, who came to Plymouth in the 1890s, lost his wife and later married Bessie Chesler of New York in 1904. Frequently, there was a large age difference between the husband and his second wife, which suggests that the marriages might have been arranged. Mayer was about forty-four and Bessie only twenty-one, while David Resnick was thirty-eight compared to his twenty-four-year-old bride. Max Toabe was ten years older than his new wife.

By the early twentieth century, young people in Plymouth chose their own spouses. Frequently, couples were introduced by an older friend or relative. Once Max Toabe remarried, his sister Sarah went to Boston to find a job, returning to Plymouth every weekend to stay with her family. Rose Sherman Geller recalled hearing how a neighbor hinted to her boarder, recent arrival Abram Sherman, that there was a pretty girl who visited Plymouth every weekend. Sarah and Abram were married in 1905. Since there was no synagogue at that time, the ceremony was held in the Red Men's Hall on Middle Street. The couple settled at 106 Sandwich Street, where their four children were born.

Max Toabe and his sister Sarah Toabe Sherman, June 1942. *Courtesy of the Sherman family.*

The Importance of Family

With a pool of about fifty families, it was possible for the first generation of immigrants to find a Jewish spouse without leaving Plymouth. Indeed, there were several marriages between Plymouth families in the early years, including Fannie Berg and Abraham Kaplow (by 1908); Esther Skulsky and David Rice (1909); Rose Greenspoon and Benjamin Dretler (1909); and William Jacob Berg and Annie Bass (1909). By the second generation, as the size of the community diminished, it became harder to find a Jewish partner. Rose Skulsky and Harris B. Cohen (1934), Lena Milner and Samuel Koblantz (1938) and Samuel Rice, one of the first generation, who married Helen Milner (1933), are some of the few examples of Jewish Plymoutheans to marry each other in the 1930s.

Generally, Jews in nineteenth-century Europe married at a relatively early age—about 20. Among the couples of Plymouth's community who wed in their old countries, men married at an average age of 23.6 and women at 20.4 years. When their American-born children married, that generation tended to wed a bit later in life. First-generation men married around the age of 26.6 and women at 24 or so. There were more opportunities for young people in America in terms of both education and employment, which could delay marriage.[91]

Occasionally, the local newspaper gave detailed descriptions of weddings. Gertrude Cohen (daughter of Julius and Mary) married Jules Goldman of Boston in 1922. The ceremony took place in Kingston Town Hall and was performed by Rabbi Borkin. "The bride wore a gown of white satin, covered with Chantilly lace and tulle bows on either side. Her veil was of Spanish lace, caught up with orange blossoms in coronet fashion. She carried a shower bouquet of white roses." After the wedding, the couple and 250 guests enjoyed a chicken dinner and dancing.[92]

Mixed marriages were almost inconceivable. "The only intermarriage was a Litvak and a Russian, or a Sephardic marrying an Ashkanazi."[93] By the 1920s, it became harder to find Jewish spouses locally, and several families moved away to make it possible for their young-adult children to marry within the faith. Dozens of young people found mates in Boston and the surrounding towns, both north and south, through a complex network of friends and relatives. Abe Penn met his wife, Ida Levine, at a wedding in Boston. Marriages were frequently announced in Boston's *Jewish Advocate*.[94]

Nonetheless, by the 1920s, a few American-born children wanted to marry gentiles. In one case, an immigrant father tried to make his American-born son marry within the faith, even from beyond the grave. The son was in love with a *shiksa* (non-Jewish woman). When the father died, he made a provision in his will that his son could only claim his inheritance if he married a girl of Jewish parentage. The young man decided to enter into a marriage of convenience with a girl with whom he'd grown up. Eventually, the couple divorced; each remarried more happily within a few years.[95]

Divorce was rare but did occur. After a business disagreement, Simon and Sarah Orentlicher decided to move their family to Brooklyn, where their children could meet other Jewish young people. Years later, one of Simon's granddaughters mused that her grandfather did not get his wish of seeing his four daughters have successful marriages—two were divorced and later remarried, and the youngest, Betty (Rebecca), had a career instead of marrying.[96]

CHILDREN

Sylvia Rubenfein Cohen with her son, Wilfred, circa 1923. *Courtesy of Gladys Cohen Rotenberg.*

Couples of the first generation of immigrants had fairly large families. In the first two decades of the century, families of four or five children were common. The Orentlichers were the largest family with thirteen children, ten of whom lived to adulthood. Generally, babies were spaced about two years apart. Without birth control, the next baby was typically born a year or so after the prior infant was weaned, as breast-feeding tended to discourage pregnancy. There are a few instances, however, in which women bore children at even shorter intervals. By the 1920s, smaller families with two or three children were more common.[97]

Shoman and Goldsmith family, circa 1912 *Standing, left to right*: Annie Shoman Goldsmith, Simon Shoman, Maurice Shoman, Mary Shoman, Betty Shoman; *seated*: Nathan Goldsmith holding son Bill, Samuel Shoman, Edith Shoman, Bob Shoman. *Courtesy of the Shoman family.*

Frequently, couples were separated for several years by immigration, as the husband went to America first to earn money to bring over the rest of the family. Elmer Berg was born a year or so after Ida Berg joined her husband, Joseph, in Plymouth. Three of the six Dezoretts children were born in Russia and three in Plymouth. The Shomans also had two children after Edith arrived in Plymouth, to join the four who had come from Russia. Often the American-born children received more education and opportunities than their elder siblings.

In the early years, children were born at home. Rose Sherman Geller remembers hearing about her home birth in 1918. Neighbor Rocheh (Rachael) Resnick called Dr. Hitchcock, who came to deliver her. Milton Penn was born at home in 1923. Some mothers employed local women, like Fannie Pyzanski, to assist in delivering babies, as she was known for her high standards of cleanliness. By the 1930s, though, most children were born in the hospital.[98]

Children were named for deceased relatives, particularly grandparents. Typically, boys were named at their *bris* (*brit milah*, or circumcision), while girls received their names soon after birth, when their fathers were called to the bimah to recite Torah blessings. Sometimes American-born children received traditional names, like Fannie or Abraham, but later changed them to American names like Frances or Faye and Alvin. Eventually, parents gave their children American names based on traditional names. For instance, Melvin Klasky, who was born in 1928, was named for his grandfather, Mendel.[99]

Not all children reached adulthood. Death from sickness or accident was more common than today, particularly among the first generation of immigrants. Three of Sarah Orentlicher's babies died young, as did the Basses' daughter Becca, who was born and died in 1899. Libby (Leah) and Jacob Sadow survived a terrible tragedy—while living in Manchester, England, their three-year-old daughter Anna was "standing in front of an open fireplace, and her dress caught fire." She died of the burns. Libby could not stop crying, and Jacob decided to move from England to take her away from the scene of the tragedy. After living a couple of years in Plymouth, Libby gave birth to another daughter, whom she named Anna in memory of her other child.[100]

At least one child was developmentally challenged. Ralph Jacob Resnick, son of Morris and Celia, was known throughout Plymouth for his love of sports and his sweet nature. An avid sports fan, he went to every school ballgame, whatever the weather. Ralphie carried water for the kids, accompanied the teams on road trips and helped the injured. Every schoolchild in Plymouth knew him, and the local sportswriter referred to him as a "living institution." Mel Klasky recalled shooting baskets with Ralphie. Although he shot underhand, he kept up with the other players. After Ralphie's death at the age of thirty-eight, the local Little League dedicated a trophy in his honor.[101]

Education

Almost all children were educated through grade school. In Plymouth, children attended one of several public elementary schools within walking distance of their homes. Those who lived on Summer Street attended the Cornish-Burton School, those nearer the waterfront went to the Nathaniel Morton School, etc. As Plymouth's Jewish population was quite small and did not make up the majority of any neighborhood, children were educated in an integrated environment with Protestants and Catholics. Some boys, particularly the older ones, stopped going to school around age fourteen in order to work, either for the family store or in the mills. Their income helped provide for the family.

There was only one high school, and young people from all neighborhoods in Plymouth attended the new facility on Lincoln Street, built in 1892 (today Plymouth's Town Hall). In the early 1900s, the school offered an elective system with four tracks: classical, science, literature and commercial. Sue Sadow chose the classical college-prep track. She had considered the commercial course but did not want to end up as a bookkeeper for the family store. In her autobiography, Sadow described her graduation in 1913, when her mother made her a white dress with white gloves. The ceremony was held in the school's largest meeting room, emptied of desks and filled with chairs. Boys and girls entered from different sides of the room and then ascended a platform to receive their diplomas and roses.[102]

Many young people left school at that point to work. Some boys, however, particularly younger sons, were able to continue into college and become professionals. Max and Celia Sadow's elder sons, Philip and Laurence, both joined the family trade and soon opened their own clothing shops. Younger son Alvin, however, stayed in school and attended MIT. Solomon Dezoretts, born in the Ukraine, worked with his father, Israel, at the Plymouth Foundry, while the younger son, David, who was born in America, went on to college.

Advertising sign for Sadow's Men's Shop. Laurence Sadow, son of Max and Celia Sadow, ran a men's store, the Wardrobe, on Main Street in Plymouth, Massachusetts, from the mid-1920s until the mid-1930s, when he and his wife, Ruth, relocated to New Bedford. *Courtesy of Bill Fornaciari.*

He attended City College of New York (known as the Jewish Harvard) and then St. John's Law School.

Some families who were well established, particularly the earlier arrivals, were able to send several of their children to college. Russian-born Kebe Toabe attended MIT, while his American-born brother Igo William Toabe went to law school. Their sister Irene Toabe received an MA in social service from the University of Chicago. Louis and Ida Resnick's sons Maurice and Albert both became lawyers, while their brother Harry worked as an accountant.

Selig (Philip) Steinberg attended Harvard University, where he studied economics. While he started at Boston University during World War I, Cordage Company executive William Hedge urged Selig to transfer to Harvard. Hedge, a Harvard alumnus, suggested that Selig apply for the Sever scholarship and served as one of his references. Upon graduation in 1920, Selig had no leads for employment. One day, while sitting on a park bench in Boston Common, he met a newspaper owner. The two men chatted, and Selig was offered a job as a reporter for the *Greenwich* [Connecticut] *Press*. By 1925, Selig had moved to the *Springfield Republican*, where he worked as the farm and garden editor. Selig enjoyed a long, successful career as a newspaper columnist and publisher, ending up as a finance writer and consultant in New York City.[103]

Although it was unusual for girls to go to college in the early twentieth century, a few did. Sue Sadow had a fight on her hands to convince her family that she should go for further education. "A *girl* get more education? Why? A *girl* gets married and raises a family," her aunt Ida scolded her. Sue had done very well in school, and her high school principal recommended that she attend Simmons College in Boston, which she did, focusing on social work. Sue wanted to "get more education and see the world." Sue's younger sister Helen followed in her footsteps. Even a generation later, when Rose Sherman Geller went to the University of New Hampshire, it was still not common for Jewish girls to go to college.[104]

Jewish education was the purview of the synagogue. Boys went to *cheder* at the synagogue to study Hebrew and scripture. Rose Sherman Geller recalled learning Hebrew as well, both at home and at the synagogue. Unlike today, becoming a *bar mitzvah* was not a major event. Neither Rose nor her mother Sarah attended her brother Hy Sherman's *bar mitzvah*. Abram Sherman took his son to Rabbi Jacob Korff's synagogue in Boston. "There was a *minyan* and some schnapps. That was it," she recalled.[105]

Death

When emigrants left Europe, they took the chance that they might never see their families again. Max and Jacob Sadow's mother stayed in Doag, Lithuania. Only one unmarried son, Julius, who lived in Boston, was able to visit her in Europe. Shortly after he returned, the family heard that she had died:

> *My father stayed home from the store for a whole week, which meant my mother had to go there all day long. He was sitting "shiva"* [seven days of mourning] *at home…He sat on a low stool, was in his stocking feet, prayed all day, and looked sad. Each morning when it was still dark at six o'clock…nine Jewish men arrived in their working clothes…They came to say the prayer for the deceased…My mother prepared glasses of tea to serve them before they left…The same group arrived at sundown every day for the week of "shiva."*[106]

Sadly, death at a young age was not uncommon. The immigrant generation worked hard, and some worked themselves to death. Tailor Samuel Shoman died suddenly from a brain tumor in 1920 at the age of forty-nine. David Resnick dropped dead in Boston at age fifty-seven the next year. Even surgery was risky. In 1933, Ida Kabelsky suffered a fall. She underwent surgery and died from cardiac arrest, leaving her husband, Frank, and four teenage daughters. Work conditions could be dangerous as well, and one member of the Jewish community, Lewis Smith, was killed in an accident at the Plymouth Cordage Company in 1918.[107]

Frank Kabelsky in front of the family home on South Street, circa 1920. *Courtesy of Nancy Kabelsky Cutler.*

It is not known if there was a *chevra kaddisha* (burial society) in Plymouth to help prepare the deceased for burial, but in the early years, people were laid out in their homes rather than in funeral chapels. In 1930, Abram Sherman entered the hospital for surgery and died suddenly of an embolism at age forty-eight. Daughter Rose Sherman Geller, only eleven years old at the time, recalled standing crying in the hallway of their house on Lothrop Street, where the family had moved from Sandwich Street. According to custom, he was laid out on the parlor floor of their home. Sherman's death was a shock to the Jewish community. Not only was he young, but he was also a successful businessman and community leader. Rose remembered the men of the local Jewish community marching in front of the hearse.[108]

Young men were at risk from war. Fifteen men of Plymouth's Jewish community, both foreign and native born, served in World War I. At least one, Samuel Smith, son of Louis and Ida Goldberg Smith, was killed. Born in Russia, Smith worked for the Plymouth Cordage Company prior to enlisting in the army during the border conflicts with Mexico in 1916. He enlisted in the Standish Guards and served in the 101st Infantry in France, where he was killed on August 8, 1918.

The Jewish community was also impacted by the worldwide Spanish influenza epidemic of 1918, which was responsible for more deaths of Americans than the First World War. The virus attacked people in their prime and claimed the lives of seventy-three Plymouth residents in a couple of months. One victim was Mitchell David Cohen, son of Julius and Mary. He had lied about his age to join the army and survived World War I, only to fall to the dangerous flu just before his eighteenth birthday. Harris Kaplowitz, who ran a clothing store, also succumbed to the epidemic at age forty-seven or so.[109]

Plymouth street directory advertisement for Harris Kaplowitz's men's clothing business, circa 1913.

There was no Jewish cemetery (or section of a cemetery) in Plymouth until the 1970s, so the town's Jews were buried either in nearby Brockton or in the Boston area. Brockton, located about twenty miles northwest of Plymouth, had a substantial enough Jewish population by the turn of the century to establish Plymouth Rock Cemetery on Pearl Street. Michel Toabe, who died in 1906, was probably the first of many of Plymouth's Jews to be interred there. Others, including Samuel Medved and Max and Celia Sadow, were buried at Adath Jeshurun in Roxbury. Village ties were more important to other members of the Sadow family, many of whom are buried in Anshe Dowag (son of the village of Doag, Lithuania) in West Roxbury.

Extended Families

Jews frequently moved to a city or town because they had relatives there, and Plymouth was no exception. Many families were interrelated. For instance, Sarah Orentlicher and Rebecca Dezoretts were sisters, which may have been a factor in the Dezoretts family's decision to settle in Plymouth. Abram Sherman was connected to two families through his sisters—one was Barnet Skulsky's mother, and another was married to John Padlusky. Rose Sherman Geller recalled celebrating several holiday dinners with the Padluskys.

Sometimes families were connected through both marriage and their village of origin. Friends Abram Sherman and Meyer Shwom both came to Plymouth from Dubno (Ukraine) around 1903, and Meyer's brother Ellis joined them a couple years later. The Shwom brothers ran a clothing store in North Plymouth across the street from Sherman's hardware store. Ellis Shwom's wife, Stella Stein, had a brother, Isaac, in Plymouth. To make things even more complicated, the woman Meyer married, Rose Berger, was the sister of Max Toabe's first wife, the sister-in-law of Abram's wife, Sarah Toabe Sherman!

The best example of family chain migration to Plymouth is the Resnick "clan." Brothers Louis and David were the first to settle in Plymouth, followed by sister Ida Resnick Goldberg. Nephews Morris Benjamin and Simon and niece Gertrude Resnick (Collier) joined them. The Resnicks were close, and when David's first wife died, nephew Morris B. and his wife, Celia, helped raise the two sons. They were also prolific. In 1917–18, no fewer than six male Resnicks registered for the draft in Plymouth. By the 1920s and '30s, the children of the first generation had begun to marry, and the Resnick extended family in Plymouth grew rapidly.

In at least one case, family quarrels became public. Morris B. and Simon Resnick were brothers and had gone into the cattle business together. After a disagreement, the two split. Community members recalled the two brothers arguing at services—sometimes shaking fists at each other from opposite sides of the sanctuary.

Many of the first generation of immigrants were lucky enough to know their children's children. Rebecca Shriber lived with her daughter, Gertrude Shriber Klasky, and her family on Union Street. Mel Klasky, the youngest grandchild, took care of his grandmother, escorting her to synagogue every Saturday, into town and to the movies.[110]

Celia (Tsvia) Resnick's grandchildren recalled family celebrations at the 88 Sandwich Street house, when she made her famous sponge cake and sweet-sour tomato soup with meatballs. She would squeeze her grandchildren's

faces with her long fingers, exclaiming, *"Shena punim"* (pretty face). Bernard Resnick fondly recalled visits to grandparents Louis and Ida Resnick with his brother Stanley. Other cousins came—Bernard Shulman from New York and Maurice's children from Connecticut—to join Ben and Ruth Resnick's family in Plymouth. Ida picked blueberries with her grandchildren and tended her large garden at the rear of the family house at 92 South Street. She also kept chickens and ducks and sent each of her children's families a freshly slaughtered duck for Thanksgiving dinner every year.[111]

Celia Resnick, circa 1950. *Courtesy of the Resnick family.*

Some of Louis and Ida Resnick's grandchildren, circa 1930. *Back row, left to right*: Robert Resnick, Bernard Shulman and Stanley Resnick. *Front row, left to right*: Laura Resnick and Miriam Resnick. Robert and Laura's parents were Ben and Ruth Romanow Resnick. Bernard is the son of Louis and Lillian Resnick Shulman, and Stanley and Miriam were Maurice and Sarah Wainer Resnick's children. *Courtesy of the Resnick family.*

While the Jewish people had close family ties within their community, they were part of a larger, ethnically diverse town. They lived, worked, went to school and played in a gentile society and embraced Plymouth's historic heritage.

Chapter 6

A Community within a Small Town

JEWISH PLYMOUTH

In *How Strange It Seems: The Cultural Life of Jews in Small-Town New England,* Michael Hoberman explores how towns like Laconia, New Hampshire, and North Adams and Great Barrington, Massachusetts, proved good places for Jewish people to live. While some of his informants did encounter anti-Semitism, generally Jews were among other newcomers. They were able to prove themselves through hard work and become accepted in their communities.[112]

Plymouth was a good place to live. In the early twentieth century, the town was growing rapidly—the population grew from 9,592 to 13,045 between 1900 and 1920. Industries like the Plymouth Cordage Company and the woolen mills attracted immigrants from Italy, Portugal and Germany. The two largest town centers, Plymouth and North Plymouth, provided opportunities for Jewish retailers and tradesmen. The rapidly growing population required housing, and Jewish property dealers provided inexpensive apartments from converted older homes. Cranberry farmers in the rural parts of town hired workers from Cape Verde, Finland and other places to maintain their bogs and pick the fruit; these workers needed shops. Additionally, Plymouth's historic heritage provided tourism opportunities for retailers and tour guides.

While there was no single Jewish neighborhood, a snapshot circa 1920 shows that Jews tended to live in certain areas of Plymouth: Summer/High

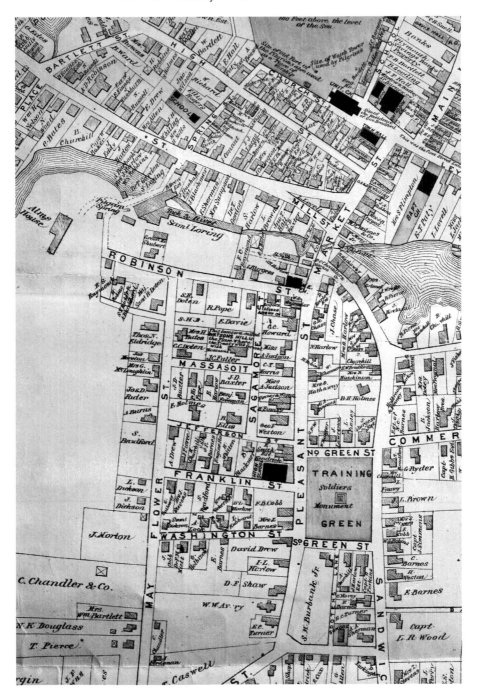

Detail, map of Plymouth, Massachusetts, J.B. Beers & Co., 1874. The synagogue is located at the intersection of Sandwich and Pleasant Streets, across from the foot of Robinson Street. Many members of Plymouth's Jewish community lived nearby in the 1920s. The building footprints shown in the map changed little until the 1960s. *Courtesy of Plimoth Plantation.*

Streets, Sandwich and South Streets in central Plymouth and Court Street in North Plymouth. With the exception of North Plymouth, these areas were within walking distance of the synagogue located at the corner of Sandwich and Pleasant Streets. These were Plymouth's older, unfashionable neighborhoods. Summer and High Streets were lined with large, often run-down, out-of-date colonial houses, many carved into tenements. Homes in other areas, like Sandwich and South Streets, were modest in size.[113]

The synagogue is located immediately south of Town Brook, which borders Plymouth's central business district. In the nineteenth century, people who lived over the brook came from "t'other side." Many Jews lived within a rectangle formed by Sandwich Street on the north, Union Street on the east, Pleasant Street on the west and South Street on the south. Sue Sadow referred to this neighborhood as "over south."[114]

The lot that Joseph Berg found for the synagogue was located at the intersection of Sandwich and Pleasant Streets. It had a small, gambrel-roofed house facing Sandwich Street and just enough space at the south end of the lot to construct a house of worship along Pleasant Street. That

House at 2 Pleasant Street, next to the synagogue, 1960. Several Jewish families lived in this house over the years, including the Dezorettses, the Frims and the Steinbergs. The house was demolished in the 1960s. *Courtesy of the Plymouth Redevelopment Authority.*

dwelling was rebuilt circa 1910 and then demolished during urban renewal around 1965. The house that used to be on the synagogue's lawn was long occupied by Jewish families, first the Dezorcttses and then the Steinbergs. Down the street to the southeast (where Dunkin' Donuts is today) lived tailor Benjamin Dretler and his wife, Rose. The Shomans lived across the street in an old Cape Cod house with Town Brook at the bottom of their backyard.[115]

A few families lived east of Sandwich Street close to the waterfront: Water, Union and Bradford Streets. They included the Orentlichers and Rappoports on Bradford Street. The Shriber/Klasky family lived on Union Street, with a house on one side and a barn for their antique furniture business across the street. Mrs. Abraham Frim lived a few doors north. The Glassmans' house/cigar shop was located at the intersection of Water and Sandwich Streets. Mrs. Sarah Glassman cooked for some of the single men in the community, including Reubin Winokur and Julius Sepet. She was known also for her excellent baking, especially her apple turnovers.[116]

Across from the synagogue, extending west from Pleasant Street was Bass Alley, which ran along the south side of Town Brook. The lane,

View southward along Pleasant Street, 1960. The synagogue is at the left. The house in the center was owned by Kasiel Simon Bass at the beginning of the twentieth century. Bass Alley runs in front of the house, parallel to the Town Brook. *Courtesy of the Plymouth Redevelopment Authority.*

which was named after Kasiel Simon Bass, who lived there for many years, disappeared during urban renewal in the 1960s. Pleasant Street, which borders the Town Green, had many Jewish homes, including 57 and 57½. *Shochet* Jacob Steinberg ran a small grocery and butcher shop at number 57. Nancy Kabelsky Cutler remembered visiting the Steinbergs as a girl. Mr. Steinberg killed the chickens in his basement, and Nancy recalled holding the chickens' feet for him. The Julius Cohen family owned 2 South Green, which was divided into several apartments. Over the years, several members of the Cohen family lived there, including Harris and Rose Skulsky Cohen and Edward and Adele Cohen Baler, as well as other Jewish families like the Penns and Goldsmiths.[117]

A group of small houses on Sandwich Street, many occupied by more than one family, formed a Jewish nucleus: 105, 106, 106½, 107 and 108. On the west side, number 105 housed a number of Jewish families over time. Cattle dealer Simon Resnick and his wife, Rachael, lived there as early as 1915 through the 1930s. The Padlusky family resided next door at number 107. Ida Padlusky was Abram Sherman's sister, and her husband, John, worked for one of the woolen mills. Ida was known for her cooking, and she ran a boardinghouse for out-of-town peddlers who wanted to stay in a kosher home. Behind the Padluskys' house was the car barn for Plymouth's trolley system (defunct by the 1920s). According to family legend, the Padluskys used to keep chickens in one of the old trolley cars.[118]

Across the street, the Sherman family lived at 106 Sandwich from around 1907 until the early 1920s, when they purchased a comfortable house on Lothrop Street, just north of the center of town. The Shermans took in Jewish boarders—the 1920 census lists a furniture store clerk named Louis Kordish. In the early 1930s, the Kabelskys lived at 106½ Sandwich Street, in a house behind number 108, which was owned by the Skulskys. Another Jewish family, the Bolotins, lived adjacent. Nancy Kabelsky Cutler remembered hearing Mrs. Bolotin coaxing her daughter Sylvia to eat her oatmeal, "*Es, es, es!*" Mr. Bolotin ran a vulcanizing business at 19 Sandwich Street in later years.[119]

The neighborhood was not exclusively Jewish, but people got along. In an oral history, Plymouthean Joe Busi related how, as a boy, he used to play ball on one of the fields by the Lincoln Street high school. One day he was engaged in a ballgame when "this fellow Sherman" (probably Louis) came along. The boys knew each other from school. Busi noted that Sherman had a chicken's head sticking out of his sweater—he was on the way to the *shochet* to have the chicken slaughtered for Shabbat dinner and had to wait for the rabbi to return. Busi called his younger sisters to babysit the chicken while the Sherman boy joined the game until it was time to go to the rabbi.[120]

Immediately south of the Town Green is South Street. Just off it is Mayflower Street, where Abraham Miller established Plymouth German Bakery at number 31 around 1911. Although he changed the name during World War I, the bakery continued after he moved to Salem, run by Joseph Resnick, Isaac Goldstein and Abraham Rosenthal. They and their families lived in the house at the front of the lot and baked in a small building behind it.[121]

Proceeding southwest along South Street, the Zavalcofskys resided at number 61. A cluster of Jewish families lived on the western end of South Street, near Towns Street. Louis and

Ben and Ruth Romanow Resnick in front of the Resnick home at 92 South Street, circa 1925. *Courtesy of the Resnick family.*

Ida Resnick lived for years at 92 South Street, where they ran a grocery store. Grandson Bernard Resnick recalled a deep lot where his grandmother Ida tended a huge garden. Next door at number 90 were Ida Smith and her children, including married daughter Flora Rosen and her husband. Louis Resnick's nephew Morris B. Resnick and his wife, Celia, lived a couple doors down in the other direction at 96 South Street until they moved to Sandwich Street around 1924. The Goldbergs, also Resnick relations, lived across the way on Towns Street, not far from Hyman and Gertrude Miller at 99 South.

Moving northward over the Town Brook was Summer Street. The Summer/High Street neighborhood, extending west to include Edes and Russell Streets, was about 10 percent Jewish by the 1920s. Jews both rented and owned houses near where the John Carver Inn is today. While once a nice area, by the early twentieth century many of the homes were run-down and divided into tenements. The Markuses bought a couple lots and

North side of Summer Street, Plymouth, Massachusetts, circa 1933. The building with the balconies is 41 Summer Street, an apartment building built by the Markuses circa 1908. Several Jewish families lived here over the years. *Courtesy of Plimoth Plantation.*

erected modern two- and three-decker houses, such as the one at 41 Summer Street, occupied by several Jewish families including the Lewises and the Student brothers, Joseph and Hyman. In the early 1920s, Joseph and Sylvia Cohen opened a grocery store, National D., a few doors down the street at 27 Summer that catered to the Jewish community. They carried a variety of goods, from lox and whitefish to canned goods and kerosene. Cohen had kosher meat sent from Boston on the railroad express. Daughter Gladys remembered that when Dr. Duby came in, he always sliced his own lox, paper thin. Muriel Swartz remembered going shopping at Cohen's on Saturday. Sylvia always invited people upstairs for coffee and pastry, particularly apple pieroshkas.[122]

Sue Sadow grew up in a solid old brick house at 29 Summer Street, where her family lived until her parents, Max and Celia, built a new house at 29 Russell Street. When her uncle Jacob and family moved to town, Sue's mother, Celia, helped the newly arrived immigrants purchase a house across the street at 48 Summer. Max and Celia were well established and were known as the *reiche* (rich) Sadows, while Jacob's family were the *oremeh* (poor) Sadows. The Sadows' neighbors on Russell Street included David Resnick and family and the Alberts.[123]

Some houses or lots were multi-family, like the Kaplowitz house at 49 Summer Street, with its unusual brick ends with exterior chimneys. The Kaplowitzes lived on one floor and the Greenspoons on the other. Joseph Berg purchased several lots on the other side of the street. His family lived in a small house at number 68, overlooking Jenney Pond, and rented the larger

Kaplowitz house at 49 Summer Street, Plymouth, Massachusetts, 1960. Mary Kaplowitz and her children lived here after the death of her husband, Harris. The house was moved across the street in the 1960s as part of an urban renewal project and is now known as the Harlow/Bishop House. *Courtesy of the Plymouth Redevelopment Authority.*

house at 70 Summer to the Kaplows. Several Jewish families purchased homes at the west end of the adjoining High Street, including Rabbi Nathanson and butcher Esser Milner at number 55 and Fannie Pyzanski at number 58.

Many Jewish businessmen ran shops in or near Town Square, just northeast of Summer Street, including cobbler Louis Goldstein, as well as tailors Benjamin Dretler and Aldi Greenspoon. Kasiel Simon Bass ran a variety store at 13 Market Street, which later became part of Julius Cohen's general store. In the early 1920s, Joseph Cohen and his partner, butcher Julius Sepet, opened a grocery store on Market Street, which was patronized by all sorts of people in the neighborhood, not just Jews. Ginny Emond Davis recalled that her mother always told her to have Mr. Sepet cut meat for her when she went to the store, as he was very precise.[124]

Plymouth's business district expanded in the 1910s with the construction of a new bridge over Town Brook and a new thoroughfare, Main Street Extension, which connected Main and Sandwich Streets. Historically, Main

Market Street from Summer Street, Plymouth, Massachusetts, circa 1932. Aldi Greenspoon's tailor shop at 32 Market Street is behind the "caution" sign. *Courtesy of Plimoth Plantation.*

Street had ended at Leyden Street, as the Town Brook was quite wide at that point. The road took a jog westward, where it crossed the brook at Market Street. The newly constructed Main Street Extension was built on land that had been used for grazing horses by business owners with shops on the adjacent Market Street.[125]

Several new structures were built along Main Street Extension, including the post office and the red brick Emond Building. Abraham Kaplow, William Lewis and the Koblantz brothers, Hyman and Samuel, all ran tailor shops there. Around 1920, Abram Sherman divided his businesses, with a hardware store in North Plymouth and a furniture store in the Emond Building. The Feldmans, Maurice and Evelyn, ran a phonograph shop on Main Street Extension. One of the first to build a store on the new street was tailor Samuel Shoman, who had a house and shop on Sandwich Street across the street from the synagogue. When his shop burned in the spring of 1916, he built a new structure on his lot, extending diagonally from the south side of Sandwich Street eastward to

Town Brook looking westward, circa 1915. Samuel Shoman's new building on Main Street Extension is at left. Shoman's tailor shop was upstairs, with Old Colony Furniture, run by Morris D. Resnick, downstairs. *Courtesy of Plimoth Plantation.*

the new Main Street Extension. The Shoman Building (torn down in the 1960s as part of urban renewal) housed his tailor shop, where he worked with his son-in-law Nathan Goldsmith, as well as Old Colony Furniture, run by Morris D. Resnick.[126]

Julius Cohen's apartment house, the Shirley Inn, was located farther north up Main Street, where the road intersects with North Street at Shirley Square. While the Cohens had moved to South Green Street by then, Harris lived at 56 Main Street in 1919. There were several Jewish businesses along Main Street, including Abe Penn's Puritan Clothing at the same address, the Student brothers' shoe store a few doors down and William Lewis's tailor shop in the old Woolworth Building.

Court Street extends north from Main Street at the old Plymouth County Courthouse. Several Jewish families lived on Main Street, including the William Jacob Bergs and the Goulds. The Sadows had a clothing store at

38 Court Street from 1911 through the 1930s, and William Jacob Berg ran another clothing store across the street. A couple of Jewish families, including Morris D. Resnick and the Levovitches, lived on Samoset Street off Court Street.

North of Samoset Street were the Lewises and the Rubensteins. Louis and Lillian Rubenstein lived at 143 Court, a tall structure with a mansard roof. For several years, Louis Rubenstein ran Standish Clothing, an upscale shop, at this address before moving to Main Street. The Rubensteins appear to have been well-off. Not only did they own their own house and business, but the 1920 census indicates that they also had a servant, Margaret Hinckley. The only other Jewish family who had live-in help were the Feldmans; Bernard managed the stove foundry on Water Street.

A small group of Jews lived in North Plymouth, a mile and a half from the center of town. North Plymouth was a community of immigrants, particularly from Italy and Portugal, many of whom worked for the Plymouth Cordage Company. As almost all the families were of immigrant stock, people got along pretty well. Jewish families in North Plymouth included the Dreitzers, Meyer and Ellis Shwom and their families and, until 1924, the Toabes.

There were several Jewish businesses along Court Street in North Plymouth, including Toabe's Hardware, Sherman's Hardware, the Shwoms' clothing store, Dretler's tailor shop and the Steins' furniture store. Several of the buildings were built by Jewish merchants. Joseph Berg erected the current Balboni's Drug Store building, as well as the building next to it. The lower floors were shops, and the upper stories were rental property. In 1928, Abram Sherman built a three-story structure for his furniture and hardware store. Rose Sherman Geller thought that it might have been the first in Plymouth with an elevator. Across the street, Sherman's longtime friends the Shwoms built another three-story building. Both the Shwom Building and Sherman Building have their names on them and are still in use today.[127]

People of many different ethnic groups lived and worked close together. Occasionally there was teasing. Vincent (Jelly) Baietti, who worked at L. Knife's (Luigi Cortelli) store from 1929 through 1941, recalled the Dreitzers, who ran a dry goods store at 298 Court Street in the north side of Cortelli's building. Hyman Dreitzer drove a blue Dodge panel truck all over the Cape, as far as Provincetown, selling haberdashery. His wife, Zina, whom Baietti remembered as very pleasant, stayed and minded the store. Hyman was from Russia and spoke broken English. The kids in the neighborhood used to make fun of his accent. They'd run in his store, chanting, "Hyman

The Shwom Building at 305 Court Street, North Plymouth, Massachusetts, 2012. The Shwom brothers, Meyer and Ellis, ran a clothing store at this location as early as 1915. *Author photo.*

The Sherman Building at 310 Court Street, North Plymouth, Massachusetts, 2010. Abram Sherman built the structure in 1928. It is thought to have been the first building in town with an elevator. *Author photo.*

Dreitzer, Hyman Dreitzer, how much for your one-dollar overalls?" in a Yiddish accent. He'd yell at them to get out of his store.[128]

Generally, relations were quite warm. When construction was complete on Abram Sherman's building in 1928, he decided to hold a ball in the empty structure as a way to thank his patrons in the neighborhood. A local orchestra, led by Plymouthean Mauro Canevazzi, played for the event, and people still recalled the event decades later. Both Sherman's and Shwom's stores were an important part of the community, and their generous credit system helped keep people afloat during the difficult times of the Great Depression.[129]

Jewish families, particularly those who ran stores, tended to cluster around Plymouth's major streets. One family, however, lived south of town with the wealthy "summer people." Levy Mayer, a high-powered business attorney from Chicago, summered in Plymouth with his wife and daughters. They stayed in Chiltonville, a neighborhood about three miles south of the town center, as early as 1901. Wealthy Boston-area families began summering there in the 1880s, particularly Eben Jordan of the Jordan-Marsh department store, who built the Forges estate there in the 1890s.[130]

Around 1905, Mayer built an ocean-front estate, Indian Hill, near Indian Brook in the Manomet neighborhood of Plymouth. The two-thousand-acre estate featured a "mansion house," two guest houses, servants' and caretakers' homes, an electric plant and a water plant. There were both cranberry bogs and vineyards on the grounds, and Mayer sent his friends fresh cranberries for Thanksgiving. Mrs. Rachel Mayer enjoyed tending to the gardens of roses and flowering shrubs. The family and their guests enjoyed fresh trout from the brook, as well as shellfish from the ocean. The contrast between the lifestyle of the German Jewish Mayers and the Russian Jewish immigrants, both living in Plymouth, could not have been more drastic.[131]

JEWISH PARTICIPATION IN A GENTILE TOWN

In spite of a visible Jewish presence in Plymouth's business districts, Jews made up only about 3 percent of the town's population. There was no majority Jewish neighborhood, no Jewish schools, no Jewish social organizations besides the synagogue. As in other small-town Jewish communities, Plymouth's Jews had to live and work in a gentile community. They interacted with non-Jews in school, in factories and especially in Jewish-owned businesses. They were accepted by their Yankee and immigrant neighbors on several different levels.[132]

The period between about 1885 and 1924, when immigration quotas went into effect, saw the rise of anti-immigrant sentiment, as several million people arrived in America from other countries. Many old-stock Americans were suspicious of and uncomfortable with newcomers with their foreign customs. Differences in language, religion and diet made socializing between gentiles and Jewish immigrants difficult. Intermarriage was frowned upon by both sides and almost never occurred. Jews tended to socialize among themselves, which might have made it easier for Yankees to accept them as trading partners rather than social equals.

With such a small Jewish community, it was necessary for peddlers and merchants to sell to non-Jews to make a living. Peddlers interacted with gentiles pretty much on their own terms—they could work when or where they wanted and bargain as they chose. Some peddlers, like Fannie Pyzanski, worked out of a particular neighborhood, like North Plymouth, where she sold sewing supplies from a pair of suitcases. Her grandson Milton recalled that she'd peddle four or five hours a day and stop at someone's house at lunchtime to snack on a hard-boiled egg and glass of tea. Others like Jacob Berg, Max Sadow, Joseph Cohen and Hyman Dreitzer had regular routes to sell to people in nearby towns. Cattle dealers also traded with non-Jews.[133]

Making a deal was part of peddling. Richmond Talbot recalled, as a young boy in the 1940s, hearing his Yankee father bargaining with junk dealer

Rose Skulsky Cohen at her pulpit desk in Cohen's Store, Market Street, Plymouth, Massachusetts, circa 1965. *Courtesy of the Cohen family.*

Harry Frim. One offered and the other countered until Frim finally agreed to a price, sighing, "You'll make my children starve!" Young Richmond started to cry until he realized that was part of the routine—Frim's son would have been in his twenties by then.[134]

Craftsmen relied on gentile clients for their custom. Tailor Samuel Shoman "numbered a high class of customers on his list." Celia Sadow, an excellent dressmaker, operated a sewing machine in the family store to custom-make blouses and other garments for clients. Mel Klasky recalled his father working with the Yankee families in town, buying, selling and repairing antique furniture.[135]

Jewish stores—clothing, shoe and variety stores—were an important part of the wider community, selling needed goods

Harris Cohen inside Cohen's Store, circa 1965. *Courtesy of the Cohen family.*

at reasonable prices. Many offered credit and helped carry customers through difficult times. When Cohen's Store was scheduled for demolition as part of urban renewal in the 1960s, proprietor Harris Cohen wrote down what the family store had meant to Plymouth for more than four decades. Cohen's Store was:

- *a welcome spot for young married couples with love in their hearts, but no money in their pockets.*
- *a haven for average married couples with several children and a small budget…they found the item they needed in the form of an extra bed, second-hand bureau or used stove—all in good condition and at low prices.*
- *a great help to many people in disposing of hard to sell items. At Cohen's, they were able to do so and get paid for it.*

- *a great help to many civic and religious organizations…when a cane, a wheelchair, or a hospital bed had to be brought to someone. Cohen's provided the item…without any charge.*
- *handy for a kerosene lamp or a candle when electrical service is cut off, or a bag of coal or a gallon of kerosene for poor people who are cold and have little or no money.*[136]

Harry Cohen was very well read and enjoyed discussing and debating issues with his customers. One was the young Peter Gomes, a Cape Verdean/African American youth who lived a few blocks from the store. After many religious discussions, Cohen told Peter that he should become a rabbi. Peter went on to become a Baptist minister and then minister of Harvard's Memorial Chapel and Plummer Professor of Christian Morals at Harvard. Many years later, Reverend Gomes underwent a DNA test, which revealed that his Cape Verdean ancestors on his father's side actually descended from Sephardic Jews. Maybe Harry Cohen had it right after all.[137]

Many proprietors chose American names for their stores to make their businesses more welcoming to a broad clientele. Unlike other immigrant groups, Jews had little reason to want to return home, where they faced sure persecution. Jewish immigrants were quick to fit into their new communities. Jewish businessmen in Plymouth often chose names with a historic theme that related to the town's heritage for their shops. Examples include Old Colony Clothing, operated by Samuel Medved; Louis Rubenstein's shop, Standish Clothing; Morris D. Resnick's Old Colony Furniture; and Puritan Clothing, owned by Abe Penn and Achille Maccaferri. Harry Glassman made Plymouth Rock cigars.

After several years in Plymouth, a few of the Jewish immigrants had enough spare cash to invest in property. One of the earliest of Plymouth's Jews to buy land in town was Joseph Berg, who first purchased land in North Plymouth in 1893. Several women, including Bessie Markus, Sarah Orentlicher and Mary Kaplowitz, invested in rental property. Often they rented inexpensive apartments to other Jews. One man, Julius Cohen, a shrewd businessman who expanded into real estate, purchased dozens of older houses to convert into apartments. Because of his success as a landlord, banks gave him more money to buy more houses. While he lost several properties during the Depression, his family still had more than a dozen apartment buildings in the Summer/High Street neighborhood in the 1960s. Local families who were looking for an inexpensive apartment for a relative knew they could turn to the Cohens.

The fact that Yankees trusted their Jewish neighbors in business dealings is evident in the number of loans Jews received. Max Sadow told his grandsons about borrowing money from a "Yankee banker," also to develop property. The banker loaned to Sadow without a contract—he just entered the loan in the front of his Bible. When the man died, Sadow went to his widow to pay the loan. She knew nothing about any loan, but Sadow told her to look in the front of the Bible.[138]

In spite of success in business and a desire to fit in, many Jews were still perceived as "foreign." As a child in the early 1930s, Betty Covell Sander recalled coming down a hill and seeing men with

Number 289 Court Street, North Plymouth, Massachusetts, 2010. Joseph Berg ran a dry goods store in this building in 1896, and his family lived there until about 1913. *Author photo.*

long beards and long black coats. She was frightened and "ran as fast as her little legs would carry her." Jews and Yankees respected one another, but there were certain unwritten restrictions about where people lived. Jews were not encouraged to join the local yacht club or the Old Colony Club, a very traditional old Plymouth men's organization. These unwritten restrictions did not apply to wealthy German Jews, however, as Levy Mayer summered for a while in Yankee Chiltonville and joined the Old Colony Club in 1900.[139]

While the first generation faced language and cultural barriers in completely assimilating, their children had an easier time. Jewish children went to school with other local children of many different religions and ethnicities. With the large number of immigrants arriving in the United States in the early twentieth century, public schools became an instrument of

Americanization. Children learned both the English language and American customs, which they could relay to their parents. Frequently, children's best friends were not Jewish.

While friendship was fine, marriage was another matter. In the 1930s, Rose Sherman Geller's friends were mostly Portuguese and Italian. One day, she was visiting her friend's house, and her friend's mother mused, "I really like you and your family a lot, but I wouldn't want your brother to marry my daughter…I want her to marry a Catholic." Rose was not offended—Jewish parents felt the same way.[140]

The second generation was more able to participate in town life than their parents. William Resnick, son of David and Sarah, took a job as an accountant with the local movie theater and eventually managed it during the difficult Depression years. Resnick was one of the first to participate in local fraternal organizations such as the Improved Order of Red Men (IORM). Abe Penn was involved with the Red Men and the Elks, as well as being a charter member of the local Rotary Club.[141]

PATRIOTISM AND WORLD WAR I

Both the first generation of immigrants and their children were patriotic and proud of their new home in Plymouth. During the Mexican conflict of 1915–16 and World War I, Plymouth's Jewish community participated actively in the war effort. In an era when sauerkraut was renamed "liberty cabbage," Plymouth's many immigrants were eager to show their patriotism for their new country. Some businesses changed names. Abraham Miller ran a bakery from circa 1911 to 1919 at 31 Mayflower Street. According to street directories, in 1915 it was called Plymouth German Bakery, but it was soon renamed Plymouth Bakery after the United States entered into World War I.

During the war, other businesses held flag-raising ceremonies, complete with patriotic songs, like Sadow's Women's Shop at its Court Street clothing store. In 1918, the synagogue and the Plymouth Zionist Organization held a flag raising, with a service flag featuring fifteen stars for Plymouth's Jewish young men serving in the armed forces. Two Sadows were among them—Philip and Louis. Philip enlisted in 1917 and was stationed for the next two years in Florida, where he rose to the rank of second lieutenant. As officers were expected to purchase their own clothing, Phil ordered his through the family store. His father claimed that Phil had a better overcoat than General Pershing![142]

In October 1918, Phil's cousin Louis wrote a letter home from France, where he served in I Company, Twenty-third U.S. Engineers:

> *It makes me homesick to think that I am far away from home and friends. The weather here is very different from our October days, and I have only seen the sun two days during this whole month…On Sept. 1 I ran across the "boys from home" in the 101ˢᵗ Infantry. They sure were a happy lot, and, believe me, they had seen some rough times…*
>
> *I have been inside of the city where the French lost 500,000 and the Boche 300,000. The city itself is nothing but ruins and what a shame…By the time you receive this letter it will be Thanksgiving. Last year on Nov. 30 I was playing our last game of football. Gee! "them was the happy days." All that I hope is that this war will be over and everyone home and happy a year from today.*[143]

One of the first to enlist was Elmer Bcrg, who served both in the 1916 border conflicts with Mexico and in Europe in World War I. He was a mechanic in the service and learned electronics. After he returned, he was often called upon to fix Plymouth's stoplights. The youngest to serve was Mitchell David Cohen, who apparently lied about his age to join the army. He worked in the medical department in Delaware and New Jersey. Discharged in 1917, he perished during the influenza pandemic of 1918, just before his eighteenth birthday. Two young men,

Elmer Berg in uniform, circa 1916. *Courtesy of Joan M. Tieman.*

Louis Orentlicher and Meyer Resnick, enlisted in the U.S. Naval Reserves and were activated during the war. Selig Steinberg, a student at Harvard, joined the Students' Army Training Corps but was not activated.

Several served in the army, including Sol Dezoretts and Benjamin Orentlicher, who was a member of the 5th Infantry, 20th Field Artillery Regiment. At least five men—Elmer Berg, Joseph Cohen, William Resnick, Samuel Smith and Maurice Shoman—were in the 101st Massachusetts National Guard and sent to France as part of the American Expeditionary Forces. Smith was killed in France on August 8, 1918. Shoman received a Distinguished Service Cross and the Croix de Guerre for bravery near Verdun. "After killing many of the enemy, he was left alone in a shell hole with no more ammunition. Finding himself surrounded by a sudden counter-attack of the enemy, he grabbed a light machine-gun and held off the enemy until he was rescued by his comrades. The fire from his gun was decidedly instrumental in overcoming the counterattack." He was discharged in 1919 with the rank of sergeant. Sol Padlusky also served overseas. His parents were so grateful that he returned unharmed that they paid off the synagogue's second mortgage.[144]

LINKS TO THE PILGRIMS

As Plymouth recovered from World War I, residents looked forward to the 300th anniversary of the Pilgrims' landing, an event that brought national attention to the town. To prepare for the celebration, Plymouth received both state and federal money to redevelop the town's waterfront. Water transport had declined at the harbor, leaving old wharves and run-down warehouses. In 1920, the town tore down dozens of houses, warehouses and wharves and replaced the area around Plymouth Rock with a series of landscaped parks. One of the few industrial buildings that remained at the waterfront was the stove foundry.

The highlight of the celebration was the pageant that reenacted the Pilgrims' landing, held at the new parkland on three weekends in July and August 1921. Hundreds of Plymouth residents, both Yankees and immigrants, enthusiastically participated in the spectacle. *The Pilgrim Spirit*, written by George P. Baker, celebrated Plymouth's founding in scenes depicting early explorers, the Pilgrims in England and the Netherlands and the Pilgrims in America. The leading roles were generally played by Yankees, while crowd scenes were filled by residents of all origins from all over Plymouth and nearby towns.

Several Jewish Plymoutheans acted in the pageant. Generally they were young—between the ages of thirteen and twenty-five—and born in America. Harry Resnick (son of Louis and Ida) and Israel Markus played the roles of sheriff's men and English citizens and soldiers. Four teenagers—Abraham Goldberg, David Kaplowitz, Albert Resnick and Rebecca Orentlicher—participated in the "March of the Dutch Cities of Charity." Some of the most important roles besides named Pilgrims were Indians, representing the native Wampanoag who interacted with the early colonists. The Indians were played by members of the local Accomack chapter of the Improved Order of Red Men, including William Resnick and J. Goldstein. Mitchell Toabe recalled carrying a flag in the parade of states and territories that closed the pageant.[145]

Several Jews even worked in Plymouth's growing tourism industry. Jacob Sadow's son Joseph peddled Plymouth souvenirs to tourists at the 1921 Tercentenary Pageant. Items included a self-published pamphlet on *Ye Quaint Inscriptions of Ye Burial Hill of Old Plymouth, Mass.*, which he sold for fifteen cents. Tourists arrived at Plymouth's waterfront by steamboat, and boys like Bob Shoman waited around Plymouth Rock to act as tour guides.[146]

In 1924, the Plymouth Cordage Company held a writing contest for local high school students on the topic "What Does the Plymouth Cordage Company Mean to this Community?" The winner, judged from more than ninety entries, was Albert Resnick, son of Louis and Ida. The prizewinning

Plymouth Rock at Plymouth's waterfront, circa 1905. Steamboats with tourists docked at the wharfs in the background. Local youths, including Bob Shoman, waited around the Rock to offer tours. *Collection of author.*

Plymouth Rock, circa 1922. The town demolished the old wharfs and erected the current canopy over the rock in 1920 in preparation for the 300th anniversary of the Pilgrims' landing. *Courtesy of Donna D. Curtin.*

essay was published in the business's newsletter, *Plymouth Products*. Albert starts his essay with the Pilgrims and then relates them to the Cordage Company's impact on the town. Resnick goes on to cite the Cordage's efforts in naturalizing immigrants, housing employees and encouraging literacy and sports in the community.

> *A few hundred years ago a small, storm-driven bark, crowded with men, women and children, sought shelter in a little, rocky harbor. Here they established a colony which was known for its principles of honesty, fairness and justice which enabled it to persevere through all difficulties. In 1824 a company was founded which placed its faith in those same great principles which had enabled the Pilgrims to endure all. And by these ideals the Plymouth Cordage Company has placed Plymouth on the same basis commercially that that band did historically.*[147]

Thirty-five years after his parents immigrated to Plymouth from Russia, Albert was writing about the ideals of the town's founders and receiving an award from the leader of the largest factory in town. The principles that Albert cited enabled not only Plymouth to persevere but his and other Jewish families as well.

A Community within a Small Town

Between the 1880s and 1930s, the first two generations of Jewish immigrants adapted to life in their historic new home. They established a congregation, built a synagogue, formed families and ran their own businesses. By the time the second generation came of age, the community had shrunk as residents moved to larger cities. The children of the founders faced many challenges in maintaining the congregation through the Great Depression and World War II.

Chapter 7

The Second Generation Comes of Age

The Great Depression through World War II

By the late 1920s, Plymouth's Jewish population had started to decrease. Many of the founders, including David Resnick and Abram Sherman, had died, and both Rabbi Abraham Nathanson and *shochet* Jacob Steinberg passed away in 1926. Some families, like the Orentlichers and Shomans, moved to larger Jewish communities in New York. The Markuses left for Brockton. As the second generation came of age, young people often moved away in search of new opportunities. It became harder for families to find their children Jewish partners. While a few new families trickled into town between the late 1920s and World War II, "community activity was at a standstill." Without the energy of the first generation of founders, it was left to their children and a few newcomers to reinvigorate the community and synagogue during the difficult years of the Great Depression and after.[148]

ASSIMILATION AND THE SECOND GENERATION

While the first generation of immigrants often maintained their traditional ways, they raised their children to be Americans. Parents seldom spoke to the younger generation about life in Russia, nor did they make an effort to teach them Yiddish. "Yiddish was spoken when parents didn't want their children to know what they were talking about," Milton Penn recalled. The kids probably understood more than their parents thought![149]

Education and hard work were seen as keys to success. Fathers and mothers toiled night and day to build successful businesses. They saved whatever they could to scrape together enough money to buy a house of their own, often taking in boarders to help pay the mortgage. When they could afford it, they sent their children to high school and sometimes college or business school. As a result of the determined efforts of the first generation, a class of young Jewish professionals began to emerge in the 1920s. Increasingly, members of the second generation were better off financially, and more accepted socially, than their immigrant parents.[150]

One of the first Jewish professionals to establish himself in Plymouth was Abraham S. Feinberg, son of Benjamin and Etta R. Feinberg, who ran a department store in nearby Marshfield. A graduate of Bates College and Harvard University Law School, Feinberg moved to Plymouth to build a practice after he returned from the war. He rented a law office downtown, on the second floor of the Drew Building at the corner of Leyden Street and Main Street Extension. He was successful, and in 1928, Feinberg was appointed a special justice of the Third District Court in Plymouth. Judge Feinberg, his wife, Jean, and their daughters lived in a house on Grant Street for many years in a pleasant new neighborhood just north of central Plymouth.[151]

There were a few Jewish physicians in Plymouth, including Dr. Isidore H. Waterman and Dr. Hyman Duby (Duberstein). Dr. Duby and his wife, Gertrude, moved to North Plymouth in the early 1930s. Dr. Waterman came to Plymouth when he married Hattie Resnick. After graduating high school, Hattie went to Boston to attend Bryant and Stratton Business College. While in Boston she met Isidore (Earl) Waterman, a young man from Chelsea who was putting himself through medical school at Tufts University. Waterman visited Plymouth while he was courting her. Since he loved the ocean, they decided to live there. The couple was married in October 1928 and set up housekeeping in a second-floor apartment in Hattie's parents' house at 88 Sandwich Street. Dr. Waterman opened an office on Main Street near Feinberg and began to specialize in maternity cases. He was appointed to the staff at Plymouth's Jordan Hospital in 1934, one of only six doctors on the staff at the time and the youngest to have ever been appointed. In the mid-1930s, the Watermans built an elegant red brick Colonial Revival home on Allerton Street.[152]

Attorney Reubin Winokur arrived in town in 1932. Born in Boston, he attended Boston University and Boston University Law School. One of his

Morris B. Resnick with grandson Richard Waterman at the Resnick home at 88 Sandwich Street, circa 1940. *Courtesy of the Resnick family.*

colleagues in law school was Albert Resnick, son of Louis and Ida, who brought him to Plymouth on visits. When Winokur graduated in 1932, during the early part of the Depression, it was difficult to find a job as a lawyer in Boston. He looked into smaller towns around the city and thought of Plymouth, as it had a Jewish community. Once he found out that Resnick was planning to join his older brother in Connecticut, he decided on Plymouth and opened an office at 9 Main Street. For the next several months, he slept on the couch in his office and took his meals at Mrs. Glassman's house.

The Winokur family, circa 1944. *Back row*: Adeline and Reubin. *Front row*: sons Lawrence and Stephen. Daughter Bonnie was not born yet. *Courtesy of the Winokur family.*

In December 1933, Reubin married Adeline Mankoff, and the couple moved to a house on Grant Street. Adeline had been studying to become a pharmacist, but once she moved to Plymouth, she ran her husband's law office instead. Her parents, Harry and Annie Mankoff, moved to Plymouth to help raise their three children so Adeline could go to work.[153]

Besides physicians and attorneys, there were three dentists who settled in Plymouth around 1940: Dr. Sam Hirson, Dr. Myron Policow and Dr. Harry Keller. Israel Harry Keller was born in Chelsea, Massachusetts, in 1913. His father was a cabinetmaker in a furniture factory, and Harry grew up learning to work with his hands. At the age of thirteen, Harry borrowed his father's tools to carve a rabbit that he made into the base of a lamp. His father was so impressed that he urged his son to "go to college and use your hands and your gift and your education so that you don't have to work in a factory like I do." Harry attended Bates College and decided on dentistry as a career because it allowed him to use his manual skills. After his graduation from Harvard Dental School in 1940, Harry decided to open a practice in Plymouth. He'd seen Plymouth while driving to the Cape and "fell in love with the community." Not only was it beautiful, but it also had a synagogue. He opened an office in North Plymouth, above Balboni's Drug Store. The first year, business was so slow that sometimes he went downstairs to work at the soda counter![154]

In spite of the growing number of Jewish professionals, Plymouth remained a modest community. Other newcomers came to town to work in retail or establish businesses of their own, including several members of the Arons family from Utica, New York. Robert, the eldest, had to leave school during the Depression to help the family. He found a job in the wholesale business, traveling around New York and as far as Boston. It was through his contacts in Boston that he met the Shermans and began working at their furniture store in the mid-1930s. After a few years, he opened his own furniture business. In the 1940s, he bought the Red Men's Hall building on Middle Street. His good friend Abe Penn was a member of the IORM and convinced his friend Bob to buy the building. The Aronses ran the business on Middle Street from the 1940s through the late 1980s.[155]

Three of the other brothers followed Bob to Plymouth, starting with Sam, who opened a wholesale tobacco and candy business on Nelson and Court Streets. Harry and Sidney were drafted, and Bob promised that if they returned safely, he would help get them started in Plymouth. Harry opened a dry cleaner's from the basement of his two-family house on Standish Avenue, which later became Reliable Cleaners on Sandwich Street. Sidney

Number 315 Court Street, North Plymouth, Massachusetts, circa 1940. Dr. Harry Keller's office was on the second floor. *Courtesy of the Keller family.*

worked for Bob at the store as a collector. People paid on time, and the collector visited each week to pick up their money. Another relative, Manny Arons, joined them working in the furniture store. Manny and his wife, Lucille, also lived on Standish Avenue, and Manny was a devoted member of the synagogue, serving as treasurer for decades.[156]

Arons Furniture, Middle Street, Plymouth, Massachusetts, circa 1950. The building was formerly owned by the Improved Order of Red Men, which used the second floor as a gathering space. Prior to the construction of the synagogue, the Red Men's Hall was one of the places where the Jewish community met for holiday services. *Courtesy of Bruce Arons.*

Opposite, bottom: Resnick family at the wedding of Mildred Resnick and Louis Segal, 1934. *Standing*: Earl Waterman, William Resnick, Lou and Mildred Segal, Ralphie Resnick, Alton Resnick; *seated*: Hattie Waterman, Celia Resnick, Morris B. Resnick, Irene Resnick. *Courtesy of the Resnick family.*

William Zall and his wife, Jeannette, moved to town from Quincy in the mid-1930s to run a wholesale candy business. He set up shop in the Emond Building, a multi-story brick structure overlooking the Town Brook on Main Street Extension. Other Jewish merchants had space there, including several tailors, and the Shermans ran a branch of their hardware store in the building. Daughter Ina Zall Cutler recalled spending most of her free time as a child in either the Emond Building or next door watching movies at the Old Colony Theater. Besides running a business, Mr. Zall played softball. Several of the local business owners teamed up to form a softball league. Zall was captain of Zall's All-Stars, which included Jewish members such as Myron Policow, Bob Arons, Harry Keller and Reubin Winokur, as well as gentiles from many backgrounds.[157]

The Second Generation Comes of Age

Zall's All-Stars softball team, circa 1941. *Back row, left to right*: Talbot Cobb, Richard Wirtzburger, Joseph Andrews, Dr. Myron Policow, Mr. Raymond (right background); *middle row*: Bob Emond, Richard Correa; *front row*: Robert Arons, Reubin Winokur, William Zall. *Courtesy of Ina Zall Cutler.*

Other families who came to Plymouth in the 1930s and early 1940s include the Banders, who ran Bander's Women's Apparel at 54 Main Street; Benjamin and Beatrice Moskoff, who had a meat market on Court Street; and the Romanows, whose sister was married to Benjamin Resnick. Edward Romanow worked as a mechanic at Resnick's filling station. Morris Stern worked as a lawyer but also ran a store on Main Street with his wife, Beatrice, called Carroll's Cutrate. Several newcomers married into Plymouth families, like Edward Baler, who married Adele Cohen and worked in the insurance business. Mildred Resnick married Lou Segal, who ran the Dexter Shoe Store in town. Their daughter Paula recalled that when he saw townspeople at parades and other events, he'd instantly remember their shoe sizes.[158]

The Great Depression

At the end of the 1920s, Plymouth's economy was healthy. In December 1929, the Plymouth Cordage Company reported an 11 percent profit and declared extra dividends. The Stock Market Crash of October 1929 had little direct, immediate effect on most Plymoutheans, as investing in the stock market was not a common activity for immigrants. Those with extra money to invest, like Julius Cohen and Max Sadow, bought property rather than stocks and bonds.

While few Plymouth residents invested in the stock market, the factories that employed a great deal of the town did, as did businesses around the country that bought their products. By 1931, the town was beginning to feel the economic depression. As industries suffered, unemployment increased. The town's Welfare Board began to have a difficult time keeping up with the needs of local families.

As the Depression deepened, unemployment grew worse. By 1933, Puritan Mills had temporarily closed, and the Cordage Company had been forced to decrease hours, reduce salaries and cut positions. In 1932, the Plymouth Coop Bank foreclosed on some of the land belonging to the Plymouth Stove Foundry, which was reorganized as the Plymouth Stove Works. Bernard Field (Feldman), who had managed the foundry for more than twenty years, continued his involvement, serving as treasurer. While the foundry eked by for a few years, there was little demand for appliances. In 1937, the Plymouth Coop Bank foreclosed on the stove works, which folded.[159]

Foreclosures mushroomed by 1932. The Summer Street neighborhood was hard hit. Shortly after the death of Jacob, Leah Sadow's family lost their house at 46–48 Summer Street to foreclosure. The Greenspoons, who lived at 60 Summer and rented to the Zavalcofskys, also had to give up their home. With many tenants unable to pay their rent on time, landlords like the Cohens lost some property, including one of their rental houses at 40–42 Summer Street.[160]

Concerned with the condition of the many old, bank-owned buildings on the street, Charles Strickland, a Brookline architect with Plymouth roots, along with two friends, established the Plymouth Colony Trust. The trust's purpose was to restore some of the old houses and create a historic district with shops and craft studios. Two of the properties that the trust succeeded in restoring were 40–42 and 46–48 Summer Street. The former became a ceramic studio and museum run by Miss Katharine Alden and is still in business today as the Sparrow House Pottery. Because the trust restored the two structures, they were not demolished along with most of the others on Summer Street in the urban renewal project of the 1960s.

As few people could afford to buy new clothes and other goods, merchants were hit hard, and many small businesses folded during the first few years of the Depression. A comparison of the Plymouth street directories from 1924 to 1932 is dramatic. The advertising section at the front all but disappears. Clothing businesses in particular suffered. The number of dry and fancy goods stores had decreased from sixteen to eleven by 1936.

Merchant Abe Penn, who ran Puritan Clothing, helped his store survive by diversifying into uniforms. Figuring that members of the U.S. Coast Guard and other government agencies were still being paid and needed uniforms, Penn identified a new market. He went on the road, visiting Coast Guard stations from Cape Cod and Martha's Vineyard up to Canada. Milton Penn recalled Sunday drives when his father would take the family to a seaside town for ice cream and stop at the Coast Guard station while there.[161]

One business that actually expanded during the Depression was the movie theater. In the fall of 1930, the Old Colony Theater on Main Street Extension downtown was demolished and rebuilt to become "not only a real Colonial type playhouse, but one of the future show places of this historic town." The Plymouth Theater in North Plymouth was remodeled to feature a new canopy marquis and lobby inside. Bill Resnick (son of David) managed the theater. When the old seats were removed, Resnick acquired them for the synagogue. To encourage business, he announced reduced prices in November 1931. Children paid ten cents for all shows, while adults paid twenty-five cents for matinees and fifty cents for shows after 7:30 p.m. The theater remained an important form of recreation throughout the difficult decade.[162]

Local merchants—including Shwom's clothing store, Cohen's general store, Joseph and Sylvia Cohen's grocery stores and Sherman's hardware stores—helped their neighbors by extending credit. Sylvia Cohen Rotenberg remembered that her father kept bills and customers' welfare slips in a spring device in his grocery store. When he died in 1945, Gladys and her brother Wilfred forgave many debts owed to their father.[163]

MAINTAINING THE JEWISH COMMUNITY

As Plymouth residents endured hard times in the 1930s, so did the synagogue. With the deaths of many of the founders in the 1920s, "interest lagged, and community activity was at a standstill." At one point, membership was down to twenty-four families, and only a handful of students attended the *cheder* (religious school). There were few members and even less money. Gradually, the 1913 synagogue building began to deteriorate, and there were not adequate funds to keep up with maintenance. When the steam boiler broke, there was no money to fix it, so members used a gas burner in the sanctuary and a kerosene stove to keep warm during morning services downstairs. Dedicated members like Hy and Louis Sherman repaired what they could, and the synagogue survived the Depression.[164]

Without sufficient funds, the congregation could not maintain a full-time rabbi. Rabbi Abraham Goldbergh conducted services and taught Sunday school and confirmation classes but had to work in Boston as a *shochet* to make ends meet. "The first Rabbi I remember was Rabbi Goldbergh," recalled Milt Penn. "He was a kind man, hardworking, served as the *shochet*, and later commuted to Boston to work in a Kosher slaughterhouse." Congregants also helped with services. Harry Koblantz, a tailor, often led services and read from the Torah on the High Holy Days. Rose Sherman Geller remembered sitting at her dining room table on Lothrop Street as a girl, studying Hebrew with him, as well as with Rabbi Goldbergh. The local newspaper mentions the congregation a few times in the early 1930s—election of officers, a Purim party at the Red Men's hall, Robert Resnick's *bar mitzvah*—but not a lot of activity was seen. According to the congregation's twenty-fifth-anniversary program, "Rabbi Goldbergh's efforts helped, but there was need of the same indomitable spirit that was so apparent in the building of the Synagogue."[165]

Members maintained the traditional Orthodox customs of their parents. While the *mikvah* had gradually gone out of use, congregants kept kosher and refrained from working on Shabbat or the High Holy Days. Milt Penn recalled that "it was the practice to auction *Aliyahs* [being called to the *bimah* to read blessings over the Torah] for the [High] Holiday services during the service itself. The auction was conducted in Yiddish, and since writing was not allowed, pre-written tabs were placed in envelopes identified with congregants' names." The occasional holiday sermons were conducted in Yiddish.[166]

Highlights of the early 1930s included the establishment of a Jewish Young Men's Club and a women's organization. Around 1933, Katherine Toabe founded the Plymouth Jewish Women's Club. As there were not many Jewish women in town, the club invited high school girls to attend. Rose Sherman Geller reminisced that while she had many girlfriends, there were not many Jewish girls her age, and she enjoyed attending club meetings. The other teenage girls included sisters Nancy and Martha Kabelsky. At the end of 1936, the club changed its name to the Beth Jacob Sisterhood, which still exists today.[167]

Reubin Winokur arrived in Plymouth in 1932 to find an almost "defunct" synagogue. Used to the larger Boston congregations, Winokur

Summer day out, 1937. *Back row, left to right*: Margo Donovan, Evelyn Shwom, Adele Cohen, Lilyan Kabelsky, Dottie Zavalcofsky, Faye Kabelsky. *Front row, left to right*: Florence Donovan, Martha Kabelsky, Nancy Kabelsky. *Courtesy of Nancy Kabelsky Cutler.*

found Plymouth's Jewish community to be "devoid of spiritual leadership." After months of knocking on doors, members of the congregation raised enough money to hire a full-time rabbi. The leader they chose was Samuel E. Friedman from Hammondon, New Jersey. After graduating from Temple University in Philadelphia, Friedman went to Palestine to study in the seminary. There he met his wife, Zhava, who also graduated from the same seminary. Rabbi Friedman, who started work in Plymouth in December 1936, had a rare combination of energy, imagination and a modern (yet still Orthodox) interpretation of Judaism that Congregation Beth Jacob so badly needed.[168]

Rabbi Friedman

The new rabbi infused Plymouth's small Jewish community with energy, and articles from the local newspaper show a busy, vibrant congregation. The synagogue held Friday night services at 8:30 p.m., with Saturday morning services at 9:00 a.m. and a daily morning and evening service. Sunday school was offered for three levels of students, and the Young Judea group met on Monday evenings. Adults could study both Hebrew and Yiddish. The small synagogue even had a men's choir. While the rabbi led many services and served as cantor, community members also played a large role in leading some services and coordinating discussions. For example, in honor of the presidents' birthdays in February 1939, Dr. Samuel Hirson, Louis Sherman and Mitchell Toabe led a symposium on Lincoln and Washington.[169]

Rabbi Friedman maintained a balance between the traditional and the modern. He delivered sermons each Friday night, often on a contemporary, relevant topic. On June 24, 1938, around the date of high school graduation, Gladys Cohen read the Friday night Bible story, followed by Rabbi Friedman's sermon, "Failing and Succeeding," aimed at high school graduates. On another Friday night, Rabbi Friedman lectured on "Has Religion Failed?" and "The Need for Organized Religion Today" a couple weeks later. While most sermons were in English, an occasional oration was delivered in Yiddish, such as the service dedicated to the *Gemillas Chesed* Society in August 1939.[170]

High Holy Days sermons were conducted in both Yiddish (evening service) and English (daytime service). The Yiddish sermons tended to relate to traditional topics like "Weighed in the Balance," "Happy Is the

People that Understands the Spiritual Sound of the Shofar" and "Where Do We Find Happiness?" English sermons had a more contemporary feel, including "The Rosh Hashanah Spiritual Victory of Israel" and "This Seeking Generation."[171]

Prior to Rabbi Friedman's arrival, Hebrew and religion classes were not held on a regular basis. As a boy in the early 1930s, Milton Penn had learned Hebrew from his grandmother, Fannie Pyzanski, who subscribed to a Jewish newspaper. Milton became a *bar mitzvah* in the mid-1930s. The tradition was for the young man to conduct the Saturday morning service, read from the Torah in Hebrew and make a speech. As Milt spoke with a stutter, he was nervous and used to joke, "Today I am a stammer" (the traditional line being, "Today I am a man"). Fortunately, he made it through the service without stuttering. "In the mid to late thirties Rabbi Friedman was engaged and some semblance of Hebrew and religious school came into existence," Milton Penn recalled.[172]

In the late 1930s, women and girls became increasingly more active in both learning and teaching in the synagogue. In addition to Sunday school, girls could now study Hebrew with the boys. Girls as well as boys were also encouraged to present the Bible story at Friday night services. Young women of the community, including Miriam Klasky and Rose Sherman, taught at the Sunday school, and Mrs. Friedman taught Hebrew. The rabbi also reached out to adult women. In 1939, a service was dedicated to the Sisterhood, with a sermon on "The General Status of the Woman in Jewish Law."[173]

Rabbi and Mrs. Friedman shared their love of Israel with both the synagogue and the larger community. Shortly after arriving in Plymouth, the rabbi began writing a fascinating series of articles on "Life in Palestine" in the local newspaper, covering topics from traveling there to money to polygamy. Recognizing the significance of Israel to Christians as well as Jews, Rabbi Friedman welcomed the public to lectures on Palestine and other topics, an early example of outreach between Jews and Christians in Plymouth. Mrs. Friedman taught Israeli dances to the Sunday school students, and Ina Zall Cutler recalled dancing the *Horah* with her on the way to synagogue.[174]

The rabbi also maintained cordial relationships with other local clergy. In 1934, the Pilgrim Ministers Union, originally an organization of Congregational ministers established in 1829, opened its membership to clergy of all faiths. Friedman was appointed to the executive committee in 1940. Friedman was also an energetic force in the Plymouth Council of Churches.

THE GATHERING STORM IN EUROPE

Ben and Ruth Romanow Resnick at Plymouth Rock, August 1943. *Courtesy of the Resnick family.*

Jews in Plymouth were well aware of the growing anti-Semitism in Europe. In March 1933, members of the Jewish community held a meeting at the synagogue to discuss events in Germany. Rabbi Goldbergh, Reubin Winokur and Abraham Feinberg spoke, and the congregation, led by synagogue president Benjamin Resnick, adopted a petition against the atrocities against Jews to present to Secretary of State Cordell Hull. Later that year, Resnick coordinated a campaign to raise funds for the Emergency Fund for the Jews in Germany.[175]

Storm clouds continued to gather over Europe as Nazi Germany annexed Austria in 1938 and Polish Jews living in Germany and Austria were deported. After an attack on a German embassy official by a relative of one of the deportees, a series of anti-Semitic riots broke out on November 9 and 10. Nazi storm troopers and private citizens attacked Jewish homes, synagogues and businesses across Germany and Austria. Hundreds of houses of worship were destroyed, synagogue archives were seized and many Jewish citizens were arrested.

The riots, or pogroms, became known as *Kristallnacht*, or "night of broken glass," for all the buildings that were destroyed. News of *Kristallnacht* was spread to the rest of the world by horrified journalists. In Plymouth, the Council of Churches looked for a way to respond to the terrible event.

They came up with the idea of asking Rabbi Friedman to deliver the annual Thanksgiving Day sermon the next week—the first ever to have been delivered by a Jewish person. According to Church of the Pilgrimage minister Reverend Carl Knudsen, "This is our answer to anti-Semitism." It was also symbolic of the Council of Churches' esteem for Friedman, "one of the most ardent workers" in the interfaith organization.[176]

Rabbi Samuel A. Friedman at Plymouth Rock protesting anti-Semitism in Europe in the wake of *Kristallnacht*, November 16, 1938. Acme Photos. *Collection of author.*

On November 16, 1938, the twenty-seven-year-old rabbi was photographed wearing his *tallit* (prayer shawl) and *yarmulke* next to Plymouth Rock. In his words, "On Thanksgiving Day, the cloth of Judaism and the symbolic Rock of Freedom will combine to express the spirit of righteousness." The story received attention in newspapers across the nation and brought letters of praise to both Friedman and Knudsen.[177]

In his Thanksgiving Day sermon later that month, Friedman linked the Pilgrims with persecuted Jewry. "Over 300 years ago Holland accepted the Pilgrims, harassed and persecuted, and granted them a haven of refuge… Now the descendants of the old Pilgrims in Plymouth has [sic] in turn extended the hand of welcome to co-religionists of that afflicted people."

News of the council's gesture in response to *Kristallnacht* spread nationally. Both Friedman and Knudsen received several invitations to lecture and make more people aware of conditions in Germany. In December, they spoke at Temple Israel in Boston, along with a former German official. Relations between Christians and Jews in Plymouth warmed further as, later that month, the Council of Churches met at Beth Jacob synagogue for the first time.[178]

Plymoutheans were dismayed by the ordeal of the ship *St. Louis*, a Hamburg-Amerika steamer loaded with more than nine hundred Jewish refugees from Europe. In June 1939, Cuban officials refused to accept the refugees, and then they were turned away from Florida by the U.S. government. President Franklin D. Roosevelt was extremely popular among Plymouth's immigrants, but the *St. Louis* incident caused many Jews to question his motives. "Our confidence in him was shattered," Rose Sherman Geller recalled. "It was the beginning of our understanding of what was going on in Germany."[179]

At least two families escaping Europe took refuge in Plymouth. At a July Fourth children's sports program, one of the event winners was young Charlotte Rattenbach, "a refugee from the war-torn lands of Europe." The rabbi was asked to say a few words on her behalf. Instead of talking about her experience, Rabbi Friedman asked the group of children to consider "how fortunate we all are to be here today, living in America and taking part in these games of sports, instead of games of war."[180]

Relatives of a family from Plymouth's Jewish community were able to escape from Nazi Germany to Plymouth. While many of the Toabes left the Ukraine for America around the turn of the century, Aba Taub, a nephew of Max Toabe and Sarah Toabe Sherman, left Russia during the revolution and ended up in Germany. After surviving being conscripted into the German army, Aba settled in Berlin, where he opened a dairy import/export business. He married Frances (Fannie) Tannenbaum, and their first child, Susanne, was born in 1930. Susanne recalled a somewhat comfortable early childhood. That changed dramatically in 1936. Sensing that life in Germany for Jews was becoming dangerous, her parents agreed that they should leave.

Aba left Berlin to find a place for his family to resettle, forced to leave his pregnant wife and his small daughter. The next several months were chaotic and uncertain. Shortly after the birth of their son Donald, Mrs. Taub and the children left for Italy and then for Marseilles. In the meantime, Aba had arranged for them to settle in what was then Palestine, where they stayed two years. In 1938, the family emigrated to the United States and lived in Brooklyn for two years. Eventually, the Taubs moved to Plymouth, near the Shermans and the Toabes and lived briefly in the home of Aba's aunt Sarah Sherman until they bought and moved into a home with a grocery store. Decades later, Susanne Taub Dubroff, now a well-published poet, described herself as a "slump shouldered refugee" upon arriving in this country and for some time afterward.[181]

World War II

While people had long been aware of what was happening in Europe, the Japanese attack on Pearl Harbor drew Americans into the frenzy. For young people, life was turned upside down, as men were drafted and women obliged to take care of things at home.

Several members of Plymouth's Jewish community were called to war. Milton Penn served in the South Pacific on a destroyer from 1943 until 1946. Even before the war started, Hyman Sherman, Louis Stein and Jacob Shwom enlisted and went to training at Fort Bragg, North Carolina. Hyman Sherman also served in the South Pacific, while his brother Louis was a medic. Dr. Harry Keller, who had moved to Plymouth in 1940 to start his practice in dentistry, served in the U.S. Army Air Corps. The navy sent Joseph and Sylvia Cohen's son, Wilfred, to dental school. Dr. Myron Policow enlisted in the U.S. Army Air Corps and served with Eagle Squadron in England.[182]

A total of twenty-one Jewish men from Plymouth served, and all returned home. Many others who were born in Plymouth also served in the war, including Robert Resnick and Bernard Resnick. In 1942, Selig Steinberg was

Joseph Cohen and his son, Wilfred, behind the family home on Summer Street, September 1943. *Courtesy of Gladys Cohen Rotenberg.*

the assistant to the head of the Time Control Division at Camp Miles Standish.[183]

Like many other young women on the homefront, Rose Sherman Geller saw her life's plans radically altered. Having graduated from the University of New Hampshire in 1941, Rose thought she would move to Boston and "become the great social worker." Shortly before she moved into a Boston apartment to start her new career, her brother Louie, who was managing the family furniture business, pointed out that they were short of help because so many men had been drafted. "He asked if I didn't have an obligation to the family," she remembered. "Of course, I started working in the hardware and furniture store...I did everything...I did deliveries, measured

The Keller family, Adeline, Dr. Harry and daughter Jackie, circa 1945. Son Joseph was not born yet. *Courtesy of the Keller family.*

linoleum, cut window glass and window shades. I don't remember thinking about the fact I was doing a man's job. The business had to go on...I did what I had to do."[184]

While people were braced to face tragedy on the front lines, they didn't expect it at home. Two of Plymouth's Jewish families lost relatives in one of the most destructive human tragedies in U.S. history: the Cocoanut Grove fire in Boston. On Saturday night, November 28, 1942, more than 1,000 people, including servicemen, were gathered at the Cocoanut Grove Lounge in Boston when a fire broke out. Panic ensued, and due to inadequate exits, 492 people perished. One was Jeannette Zall of Plymouth, wife of William

Rose Sherman, Ruth Brown, Estelle Pokross Sherman and Sarah Toabe Sherman at the Browns' house at Nantasket Beach, circa 1943. *Courtesy of the Sherman family.*

Zall and mother of three young children. She had gone to Quincy to visit her sister and was at the club that night. Louis and Ida Resnick's oldest grandson, Stanley, and his wife of little more than a year, Alice, were also killed. Bern Resnick recalled, "It was only a stroke of fate that I wasn't there, for Stanley had invited me to be with them, but I was working at the Boston Navy yard then and I opted out of the invitation because of priority work."[185]

LIFE DURING THE WAR YEARS

As the second generation came of age, Jews in Plymouth became more assimilated and part of the town social and civic life. They maintained Jewish identity but relaxed some of the strict customs their parents had brought from Eastern Europe. Jewish Plymoutheans started running for and holding positions in the school and town government. Many participated in local country clubs and organizations, and gradually even the most Yankee social clubs began to admit some Jewish members.

As time went by, many people became less strict about keeping kosher outside the home. Mel Klasky recalled that when he worked with his father in the antiques business, they often ate out for lunch. The Colonial Restaurant was a popular spot for Plymoutheans, including several Jewish families. Not everyone kept kosher at home, either. Among the Resnick family, there is a story about the time they decided to hold an old-fashioned New England lobster boil. They had just put the lobsters in the pot when someone noticed a car in the driveway—the rabbi's! The woman of the house was so embarrassed that she hid in the kitchen pantry until he left.[186]

While young people still overwhelmingly married other Jews, there is at least one instance of conversion. Hattie Resnick Waterman had a Finnish nanny named Lillian Puukka to help with her children, Rollene and Richard. Hattie's brother Alton fell in love with Lillian, and they courted quietly for several years. Lillian underwent an Orthodox conversion, and the couple married. "Marrying out" was not common but began to occur more frequently, but when a Jewish young man married an Italian woman from North Plymouth in 1935, many members of the Jewish community were uncomfortable with the mixed marriage.[187]

By the 1940s, several Jews began to serve their community by working with the local government. In 1937, Dr. Hyman Duby ran for a three-year position on the town's board of health. He felt that there were "many reforms and new developments that should be incorporated" into the town's health policies and offered his knowledge and experience. Dr. Harry Keller worked as the dentist for the school system, and Adeline Keller served on the town's school committee for many years. Abraham Feinberg was the town counsel for Marshfield, as was William Toabe for Chatham on Cape Cod. In 1946, Abe Penn was elected as Plymouth's town constable, and Reubin Winokur was appointed to serve on the town's Advisory and Finance Committee, which advised the town meeting. Winokur was elected moderator of the Plymouth town meeting in 1964. Plymouth did not have a Jewish selectman until the 1990s, however, when Bruce Arons, son of Bob and Sadie, was elected for two terms starting in 1989.[188]

Jews also began joining secular fraternal organizations. While there were many Jewish Freemasons, before World War II, many of Plymouth's Jews were more comfortable joining lodges in Boston or other towns. Abraham Feinberg was a leader in the Duxbury Masonic Lodge. One of the more exclusive organizations in town was the Old Colony Club, founded as a local gentlemen's club in 1769. While the vast number of its members were of Yankee origins, a few Jewish professionals were admitted as members, including Judge Feinberg in 1924 and Dr. Waterman in 1930. Jack Goldman and Wilfred Cohen joined in the 1950s.[189]

Just as men of the second generation began to participate in secular clubs, so did women. In addition to serving as a president of the synagogue's sisterhood organization, Hattie Waterman volunteered at and raised funds for Jordan Hospital, where her husband practiced. She also was involved in the local women's club and garden club.[190]

Plymouth was too small a community to have parallel social organizations like country clubs, as was common in larger cities like Boston, where Jews were often excluded. The Plymouth Country Club was very inclusive in its membership, and several Jewish families, including the Kellers and the Winokurs, were members. The Eel River Beach Club, which had among its members wealthy Boston Brahmin summer folk, was less welcoming, at least on one occasion. A man from Plymouth's Jewish community recalled a rare instance of prejudice in the 1950s, when he and another boy, who happened to be Italian, were invited by a friend to swim at the club. While they were in the pool, someone came up to them and asked the two boys to leave.[191]

Renewing the Synagogue

The synagogue kept going through the war years. Shortly after Rabbi Friedman left in late 1941 for another congregation in nearby Taunton, Rabbi Israel Gerber was hired. The synagogue enjoyed a special non-religious event in 1944, when members celebrated the "final redemption of the mortgage" on March 14. The list of contributors included sixty-six families from Plymouth, Duxbury and Marshfield, as well as the Sisterhood, Plymouth chapter of Hadassah and the Plymouth Jewish Men's Club. More than a dozen of the original founders participated in paying off the mortgage for the synagogue they had built more than thirty years before.[192]

As World War II ended, Jewish servicemen returned home. Dr. Richard Shiff, son of Jacob and Fannie Shiff of Duxbury, established an optometry practice, first in Duxbury and then in Plymouth, and David Dezoretts opened law offices in Plymouth and Taunton. Rose Sherman married Dr. Milton Geller of New Bedford, who set up an optometry practice in 1948. When grocer Joseph Cohen died in 1945, his children, Wilfred and Gladys, persuaded their cousin from Boston, Morris Bloom, to take over

Morris and Celia Resnick's home at 88 Sandwich Street. The house is no longer standing. *Courtesy of the Resnick family.*

the business. Morris and his wife, Lee, moved into the upstairs apartment in Celia Resnick's home. Morris's partner was his best friend from childhood, Jack Minsky, who had recently married Harriette Klasky. Jack became a staunch supporter of the synagogue until his death in 1996.

Several Jewish newcomers decided to make homes in and around Plymouth after the war. The Carlins opened a hardware store on Court Street, and the Kusmins, who came in 1948, ran a clothing business. One of the new families was the Russos, Ray and Millie. While looking for a place to establish Ray's veterinary practice, they visited Plymouth by accident. One hot summer weekend in 1947, the couple was looking for a place in the suburbs of Boston, and Ray suggested that they visit a seaside town to escape the heat. When Millie saw the bustling waterfront, she asked Ray why they couldn't find a place like Plymouth. The postwar real estate market was tight, and it was hard to find a place to live. Finally, they found a rambling Federal-period house in Kingston that hadn't been lived in for twenty years, moved in and opened a veterinary practice next door.[193]

The arrival of so many newcomers brought more modern religious viewpoints to the community. Some new brides from big cities were dismayed to see the old-fashioned synagogue where women still sat in the gallery. Others were surprised to see that there was still a *mikvah* (although it wasn't in use). "In the city we had already modernized. I don't remember seeing anywhere where they had a *mikvah*...never did I see any structure that was so orthodox as the structure that we had in Plymouth." Several members began thinking that the first-generation immigrant synagogue needed modernizing. "When we came home from the service in '46, we had traveled, we had seen what there was to offer in other communities, we knew that something drastic had to be done to rejuvenate the whole…community."[194]

The event that sparked the movement to modernize the synagogue occurred in 1947, when, at a synagogue meeting, the building chairman asked for $500 to calcimine a wall. That was a lot of money at the time—it would have bought a car. Dr. Harry Keller, who had just returned from the service, protested the waste of money. "For the first time in a meeting I opened my mouth and said that the only thing you should do is think about remodeling the synagogue." When the chair resigned on the spot, Keller was elected as the new head of the building committee.[195]

The new committee, including Jack Golden, Joe Carlin, Dr. Myron Policow, Hy Sherman, Victor Shiff and Mitchell Toabe, met to discuss the renovation project. With the help of Keller's father-in-law, Lionel Greene, they arrived at a figure of $20,000. When someone asked, "Where is the money coming from?" Dr. Keller stood up and pledged the $500 of separation pay he'd received from the army. Myron Policow and Hy Sherman followed in donating their separation pay, and gradually the congregation raised the necessary funds.

Renovations included moving the *bimah* to the east wall, installing pews and adding an emergency exit. In the basement, the *mikvah* was removed to make room for a bathroom and a new boiler. The Sisterhood chose colored glass to replace the clear windowpanes upstairs. Their project was budgeted for $500, but the local glass company completed it for $250. The extra money provided funds to remodel the kosher kitchen. A rose-colored carpet runner in the sanctuary was the finishing touch, and the project was completed in time for Richard Waterman's *bar mitzvah*. The total cost of the project came to $22,000—$2,000 more than the $20,000 the congregation had raised—so the builder, Mr. Rand, donated the remainder. When the project was completed, Celia Resnick relit the eternal light—an honor she missed in 1913 when another member outbid her.[196]

Gradually, the congregation modernized. At first, the women's seats were moved to the main floor, separated from the rest of the sanctuary by a curtain. After a while, families began to sit together, and the balcony was abandoned. A committee established the first workable bylaws and constructed a dues schedule with Sunday and Hebrew school fees. Along with modernizing the building, members began thinking about new prayer books. Rabbi Israel Gerber (1942–44) was succeeded by Rabbi Nathan Wise (1946–50), Rabbi

Rabbi Nathan Wise and Dr. Myron Policow standing in front of the ark at the synagogue, circa 1949. *Courtesy of the Cohen family.*

Albert B. Schwartz (1951–53) and then Rabbi Elihu Elefant (1954–56). Bob Shiff recalled that in the 1950s, the coat closet outside the sanctuary was stacked with different versions of prayer books as the congregation tried out various liturgies. Eventually, the congregation declared itself Reform, although it maintained many traditional features.[197]

As the congregation grew, it purchased a parish house in 1959 and, in 1978, bought the Methodist church building on Court Street to use as a community center. In 1974, a section in Vine Hills Cemetery was purchased and consecrated so members of the Jewish community could be buried among members of their own congregation. Rabbi Laurence Silverman brought back earth from the John F. Kennedy Memorial Forest in Jerusalem for the dedication of the cemetery. While many families have come and gone, the congregation has benefited from the leadership of Rabbi Silverman for more than thirty years. In 2009, Congregation Beth Jacob celebrated its 100th anniversary.[198]

Afterword

HIGH HOLY DAYS, 2012

One hundred years after the cornerstone of the synagogue was laid, Congregation Beth Jacob maintains its links to the past. On Rosh Hashanah, Dr. Barry Meltzer, a relative of Ida Bahn Resnick, calls out the notes for his son to blow on the *shofar* (ram's horn), using a *siddur* brought from Vilna by Fannie Pyzanski's father. Descendants of the Cohens, Shermans, Shribers, Toabes and other founders sit in the congregation, along with Aronses, Kellers, Russos, Winokurs and other longtime family members. While most High Holy Days services are held at the Community Center, second-day Rosh Hashanah services are still conducted at the synagogue.

So what's so special about Plymouth? In spite of buying a community center and talking about a new modern building with a parking lot, Congregation Beth Jacob still uses its old synagogue, built by first-generation immigrants. Completed in 1913, it is a few years older than Boston's Vilna Shul, a rare survival of a synagogue built by Eastern European immigrants in 1919, now operated as a museum. In a historic town like Plymouth, change is slow, and most residents appreciate the past—not just the Pilgrims but all that came after as well. Although the town has changed considerably since the early 1900s, Jews still enjoy living in Plymouth, a town founded by the Pilgrims, another persecuted religious minority. There's a lot to be said for tradition—both Pilgrim and Jewish!

Notes

Preface

1. See books like Hoberman, *How Strange It Seems*.

Chapter 1

2. *Old Colony Memorial* [hereafter cited as *OCM*], "Synagogue Dedicated," January 2, 1914.
3. Bangs, *Strangers and Pilgrims*, 63–71.
4. Meyer, *Hebrew Exercises*, 136.
5. Dexter and Dexter, *England and Holland*, 583; Bangs, *Strangers and Pilgrims*, 324; www.americanancestors.org/pilgrim-families-moses-simonson; Bangs, "Moses Simons of Leiden," 54–55; personal communication, Jeremy D. Bangs to author, November 22, 2012.
6. Ibid., note; www.ames.cam.ac.uk/dmes/hebrew.
7. Gabriel Sivan, *The Bible and Civilization* (New York: Quadrangle New York Times Book Co., 1974), 236, quoted in Spiro, "WorldPerfect"; Peter Gay, *A Loss of Mastery: Puritan Historians in Colonial America* (Berkeley: University of California Press, 1999), 26–52, quoted in Meyer, *Hebrew Exercises*, 15; Bradford, *Of Plymouth Plantation*, 236; source for Compact, www.mayflowerhistory.com/PrimarySources/MayflowerCompact.php.
8. Bradford, *Of Plymouth Plantation*, 97.

9. Johnson, "Crime and Punishment"; Shurtleff and Pulsifer, *Records of the Colony*, 11: 57–58; Langdon, *Pilgrim Colony*, 67; Fennell, "Plymouth Colony Legal Structure"; Spiro, "WorldPerfect."

10. Fennell, "Plymouth Colony Legal Structure"; Meyer, *Hebrew Exercises*, 17; Johnson, "Crime and Punishment"; www.churchstatelaw.com/historicalmaterials/8_1_2_11.asp.

11. Meyer, *Hebrew Exercises*, 14–16. Meyer cites the 1650 date for *Of Plymouth Plantation* from Samuel Eliot Morison, as written in his foreword to Bradford, *Of Plymouth Plantation*, xxvi–xxviii.

12. Leibensperger, "Colonial Era," 3–8.

13. Ibid., 11–13; Sarna, "Jews of Boston," 3; Dalin and Rosenbaum, *Making a Life*, 9.

14. Leibensperger, "Colonial Era," 11–17; Dalin and Rosenbaum, *Making a Life*, 8.

CHAPTER 2

15. Davis, *Plymouth Memoirs*, 351, 433, 435.

16. Smith, "Israelites in Boston," 47–49.

17. Bienen, "Mayer, Levy"; *OCM*, Obituary, Levy Mayer, August 25, 1922.

18. "Century of Immigration"; Imhoff, "Civil War to the Gilded Age," 46.

19. *OCM*, Obituary, Ida Resnick, February 8, 1934. Daughter Edith Resnick's birth is listed in the 1890 vital records, although the family records indicate 1891. For proof of residency in Plymouth see Plymouth Vital Records (Town Reports), 1893 and 1897 Plymouth Street Directories; 1900 U.S. Census, Plymouth, Massachusetts.

20. Spiro, "Pale of Settlement."

21. JewishGen Communities Database.

22. Raphael, *Synagogue in America*, 45.

23. Spiro, "Pale of Settlement."

24. Sadow, *Can Do (Said Sue)*, 39; Max Sadow naturalization certificate, USDC Boston 245-33, September 12, 1899, National Archives; Robert Shiff, personal communication with author, October 10, 2012.

25. Slutsky, "Pogroms."

26. Evans, "Leaving the Homeland."

27. "European Jewish Emigration via the Port of Hamburg."

28. Evans, "Arrival of Passengers"; "Liverpool, England."

29. "Fleets, Feeder Lines, Railway Companies"; Evans, "Arrival in a North Sea Port."

30. Sadow, *Can Do (Said Sue)*, 43; passenger list, SS *Commonwealth*, Liverpool to Boston, May 8, 1902. Morris Reznik (Resnick) is second from the bottom of the list. Column 16 shows that Morris was joining his uncle David Resnick in Plymouth. Column 9 indicates that his last residence was London; passenger list, SS *New England*, Liverpool to Boston, July 17, 1902. Column 16 lists both Morris's and David Resnick's names.

31. Solem, "Steerage on Steamships"; "Ship Descriptions."

32. "Ship Descriptions." The *Carpathia* is known for rescuing survivors of the *Titanic* disaster in 1912; Solem, "Steerage on Steamships."

33. Sadow, *Can Do (Said Sue)*, 43.

34. Clapp, *Port of Boston*, 297–308; "Steamship Berths Assignment."

35. Passenger list, Celia Resnick, July 17, 1902; Rollene Waterman, personal communication, October 23, 2012.

36. Congregation Beth Jacob, "Script for 75th Anniversary Program"; Sadow, *Can Do (Said Sue)*, 27, 43.

37. Eunice Dezorett Glassberg, interview with author, August 2005.

38. Abraham Frim naturalization certificate, 1st District Court E. Middlesex, Malden, vol. 2, 932, October 16, 1905. In the 1930 U.S. Census (Plymouth), the towns of origin are listed for both Frank and Ida Kabelsky. Ida's town of origin is semi-legible but appears to be Krackenova. "Krekenava," JewishGen Communities Database. data.jewishgen.org/wconnect/wc.dll?jg~jgsys~jgcd; Glassberg, interview with author. According to his World War I draft registration, Joseph Cohen was actually from Cherepinka, about thirty-five miles northwest of Buki.

39. Muriel Swartz, interview with author, December 20, 2003; Milton Penn, interview with author, September 5, 2012. In *How Strange It Seems*, Hoberman discusses how many Jews in early twentieth-century New England ended up in a particular town because it was the end of the railroad line. Hoberman, *How Strange It Seems*, 22–23.

Chapter 3

40. Sadow, *Can Do (Said Sue)*, 29–30.

41. Toabe, Winokur and Keller, "Founders' Breakfast."

42. Ibid.

43. Davis, *Plymouth Memoirs*, 435; Sadow, *Can Do (Said Sue)*, 29; Congregation Beth Jacob, "Yiddish Ledger Translation," 17.

44. Geller, interview by author.

45. Raphael, *Synagogue in America*, 45–46, 51.

46. Congregation Beth Jacob, "Silver Jubilee Program," 4.

47. Jacob Beis Society, Incorporation papers, March 15, 1909; Congregation Beth Jacob, "Yiddish Ledger Translation," 1, 3–4, 16, 26.

48. Plymouth County Deeds, Book 1043:330.

49. *OCM*, Obituary, Joseph Berg, January 1, 1941; Congregation Beth Jacob, "Script for 75th Anniversary Program"; Sadow, *Can Do (Said Sue)*, 47.

50. Plymouth County Registry of Deeds, Book 1043:331, 1161:381, 1172:120.

51. Congregation Beth Jacob, "Silver Jubilee Program," 4; Congregation Beth Jacob, "Yiddish Ledger Translation," 8, 10, 21, 52; Raphael, *Synagogue in America*, 53.

52. Maggie Mills, "Then and Now, Congregation Beth Jacob Synagogue," *OCM*, September 22, 1988; *OCM*, "Synagogue Dedicated," January 2, 1914; Congregation Beth Jacob, "Script for 75th Anniversary Program," 5–6; Congregation Beth Jacob, "Yiddish Ledger Translation," 7, 13.

53. Geller, "Brief History of Congregation Beth Jacob."

54. *OCM*, "Synagogue Dedicated," January 2, 1914.

55. Ibid.

56. *Congregation Beth Jacob 100th Anniversary Tribute Book*. A couple of these rabbis are mentioned in the twenty-fifth-anniversary program. Approximate dates for the others come from documents that they signed. Rabbi Nathanson appears in several Plymouth street directories as a rabbi. Samuel Krinsky appears in the 1915 street directory as a laborer, living at 29 Summer Street. By 1920, he is listed as a slaughterer in the Malden census and, by 1930, as a rabbi. Krinsky's son, William L., was born in 1915, grew up in Boston and became a Lubovitch rabbi of Melbourne, Australia. See www.collive.com/show_news.rtx?id=801&alias=rabbi-velvel-krinsky-obm.

57. Joan Tieman, interview with author, December 14, 2004; Sadow, *Can Do (Said Sue)*, 44–45; Congregation Beth Jacob, "Script for 75th Anniversary Program."

58. Bartlett, *Joseph Busi of Plymouth*, 24.

59. Glassberg, interview by author. For more information about the foundry, see chapter three.

60. Cutler and Geller, interview by author.

61. Toabe, Winokur and Keller, "Founders' Breakfast"; Leila Wolfe, interview by author, December 10, 2005. See cw.routledge.com/textbooks/0415236614/resources/maps/map49.jpg for a map of the spread of Chassidism, which includes the village of Staroconstantinov in Volhynia, where Orentlicher came from.

62. Toabe, Winokur and Keller, "Founders' Breakfast"; Sadow, *Can Do (Said Sue)*, 44–45; Geller, interview by author, October 14, 2012.

63. Geller, interview by author, March 2009.

64. Klasky, interview by author, July 26, 2012; Ina Zall Cutler, interview by author, July 29, 2012. No one interviewed, with memories back to the 1920s, recalls the *mikvah* in use.

65. Sadow, *Can Do (Said Sue)*, 6–7

66. Congregation Beth Jacob, "Silver Jubilee Program," 6; Geller, interview by author, July 2001; *Congregation Beth Jacob 100th Anniversary Tribute Book*.

Chapter 4

67. Job data derived from Plymouth street directories; Sadow, *Can Do (Said Sue)*, 28–29.

68. Bartlett, *Joseph Busi of Plymouth*, 22.

69. Ibid., 23.

70. Toabe, Winokur and Keller, "Founders' Breakfast"; *OCM*, David Resnick Obituary, January 14, 1921. Deeds show that Resnick purchased land from the Plymouth Stove Foundry and provided them funds for mortgages. See Plymouth County Deeds 929:101, 1235:113, 1242:152, 1242:597.

71. Sadow, *Can Do (Said Sue)*, 45.

72. Toabe, Winokur and Keller, "Founders' Breakfast."

73. Sadow, *Can Do (Said Sue)*, 7.

74. Guthrie, "Suassos Lane." I am grateful to Carl Finer for calling this song to my attention.

75. Swartz, interview by author; Penn, interview by author.

76. Cutler and Geller, interview by author.

77. Shiff, personal communication with author; Suberman, *Jew Store*; Hoberman, *How Strange It Seems*, 117–18.

78. Penn, interview by author.

79. Ibid., December 20, 2003.

80. Deborah Cohen, personal communication with author, October 25, 2012.

81. Resnick, interview by author. The building across from 92 South Street that was used as a store was torn down circa 2008. The Skulskys are listed in the 1924 Plymouth street directory as having a business at the same location as their home at 108 Sandwich Street.
82. Bloom, interviews by author.
83. Gladys Cohen Rotenberg, interview by author, June 2004.
84. Penn, "Memories of Growing Up," 2; Klasky, interview by author, September 4, 2012.
85. Hoberman, *How Strange It Seems*, 55–56.
86. Stephen Resnick, interview by author, August 2003; Raymond Russo, interview by author, October 2003. The Skulskys sold the farm for the access road to the nuclear plant.
87. Maggie Mills, "Supplement," *OCM*, December 10, 2001; Betty Sander, interview by author, September 20, 2012.
88. In 1905, the foundry began selling land, including a sale to David Resnick (Plymouth County Deeds, 929:101). The next year, the foundry land was conveyed to Morrissey (PCD 946:260, 961:138). Feldman appears in the 1910 census as the foundry manager, living at 47 Union Street in Plymouth. His daughter Helen was born in Plymouth in 1907.
89. Glassberg, interview by author. Job data is gathered from a variety of sources, including the census and World War I draft registrations.

CHAPTER 5

90. Toabe, Winokur and Keller, "Founders' Breakfast"; *OCM*, "Joseph Berg, 93, Wife 85, Married 65 Years," April 14, 1938.
91. Goldberg, "Life Cycle." Figures for Plymouth's Jews are based on information from the U.S. censuses and Plymouth Vital Records from town reports.
92. *OCM*, March 3, 1922.
93. Congregation Beth Jacob, "Script for 75th Anniversary Program."
94. Ibid.; Penn, interview by author.
95. Plymouth County Probate Records 175:25.
96. Leanne Wolfe, interview by author, December 2005.
97. Birth data compiled from Plymouth vital records and federal censuses.
98. Geller, interview by author; Penn, interview by author.
99. Goldberg, "Life Cycles."
100. Sadow, *Can Do (Said Sue)*, 44–45.

101. *OCM*, Walter Haskell, Obituary, Ralph Jacob Resnick, June 11, 1954; Klasky, interview by author, September 4, 2012.

102. Goldstein, "High School Days."

103. Bloom, interviews by author; archival student file, Philip Selig Steinberg, class of 1920, Pusey Library, Harvard University, Cambridge, MA. Bloom frequently told the story of Selig Steinberg's career, but some of the details slightly contradict those found in Steinberg's alumni records at Harvard University.

104. Sadow, *Can Do (Said Sue)*, 64–69; Geller, interview by author, April 2009.

105. Geller, interview by author, April 2009. She is most likely referring to Grand Rabbi Jacob Korff.

106. Sadow, *Can Do (Said Sue)*, 41–42.

107. *OCM*, April 19, 1918.

108. Geller, interview by author. Milton Penn (b. 1923) recalled that the Jewish community generally brought undertakers from Boston to prepare the deceased for burial. Penn, interview with author.

109. Hunt, "'Spanish Lady' Plagues Plymouth," 69–70.

110. Klasky, interviews by author, May 1999, September 5, 2012.

111. B. Resnick, interview by author; S. Resnick, interview by author.

CHAPTER 6

112. Hoberman, *How Strange It Seems*, 102–3.

113. Data on where people lived is compiled from the 1919 and 1921 Plymouth street directories, as well as the 1920 federal census. In cases where families moved between 1919 and 1921, the address where they permanently settled is used, i.e. the Dretlers on Sandwich Street (1921), where they resided for many years, rather than on Summer Street, as seen in 1919.

114. Davis, *Plymouth Memoirs*, 204, 241; Sadow, *Can Do (Said Sue)*, 41–42.

115. An early photograph looking south along Market Street shows the gambrel-roofed structure, which was altered or replaced by the house seen in later images.

116. Klasky, interview by author.

117. Cutler and Geller, interview by author.

118. Geller, interview by author.

119. Cutler and Geller, interview by author.

120. Bartlett, *Joseph Busi of Plymouth*, 6–7.

121. The change in the bakery's name can be seen in Plymouth street directories, 1915 and 1919.

122. Goldstein, "From Pilgrims to Poverty," 190; Rotenberg, interview with author, June 2004; Swartz, interview with author, June 2004; Penn, "Memories of Growing Up," 2.

123. Geller, interview by author.

124. Virginia Emond Davis, interview with author, August 24, 2012.

125. Bloom, interviews by author. Bloom's uncle, Joseph Cohen, had a grocery store on the east side of Market Street.

126. *OCM*, Obituary, Samuel Shoman, October 8, 1920; *OCM*, March 31, 1916.

127. *OCM*, Obituary, Joseph Berg, January 1, 1941; Geller, interview with author, March 2009.

128. Baietti, interview by author.

129. Geller, interview by author.

130. *OCM*, Obituary, Levy Mayer, August 25, 1922. For information on Mayer's career, see Bienen, "Mayer, Levy"; Engstrom, "Forges of Chiltonville."

131. Masters, *Levy Mayer*, 269. I am grateful to Tom Schwartzman for this reference.

132. In *How Strange It Seems*, Hoberman discusses how small-town Jews in New England had to work much harder at maintaining their otherness than Jews in urban areas like Beacon Hill in Boston or Brooklyn. Hoberman, *How Strange It Seems*, 118–20.

133. Penn, interview by author, September 5, 2012.

134. Richmond Talbot, interview by author, July 2002.

135. *OCM*, Obituary, Samuel Shoman, October 9, 1920; Leon Sadow, interview by author, January 2003; Klasky, interview by author.

136. Cohen, "What Is Cohen's Store."

137. Peter Gomes, Sermon at Congregation Beth Jacob's 100th anniversary, May 1, 2009. www.soundtheology.org/index.php/site/bio-pg/peter_gomes.

138. Leon Sadow, interview by author.

139. Betty Covell Sander, interview by author, September 20, 2012. Milton Penn, a contemporary of Sander, expressed surprise when he heard her story, as he recalled that few local men dressed in a traditional fashion by the 1930s. Milton Penn, interview by author. The men Betty saw may have been visting for an event. James W. Baker, personal communication with author, October 6, 2012.

140. Geller, interview by author, September 9, 2012.

141. Penn, interview by author.

142. Sadow, interview by author.

143. *OCM*, "Voices from the Front," October 27, 1918; Pilgrim Hall Museum, www.pilgrimhall.org/ww1.htm.

144. Karin Goldstein, "Plymouth's Jews in WWI," *The Tent* (Congregation Beth Jacob newsletter), November 2004; homeofheroes.com/members/02_DSC/citatons/01_wwi_dsc/dsc_05wwi_Army_S.html; Geller, "Brief History of Congregation Beth Jacob."

145. *Pilgrim Tercentenary Pageant 1921 Program* (Boston: Southgate Press, 1921).

146. I am grateful to Betty Sander for calling Sadow's pamphlet to my attention. Betty Shoman Kaufman, interview by Lipset family.

147. Resnick, "First Prize Essay," 5–7.

Chapter 7

148. Congregation Beth Jacob, "Silver Jubilee Program," 6.

149. Penn, "Memories of Growing Up," 1.

150. Raphael, *Synagogue in America*, 56.

151. *OCM*, Obituary, Abraham S. Feinberg, October 11, 1961.

152. *OCM*, Obituary, Hattie Waterman, June 6, 1991; *OCM*, "Dr. Waterman Appointed to Hospital Staff," January 19, 1934; Geller, interview by author.

153. Winokur and Winokur, interview with author, Vicki Blass Fitzgerald and Ray Russo; *OCM*, "BU Graduate Opens Law Office on Main Street," March 31, 1933. Albert Resnick ended up practicing law in Boston on Tremont Street. Jackie Keller Winokur, personal communication with author, October 12, 2012.

154. Eulogy, Harry Keller, by Jackie Keller Winokur, manuscript, 2009. Balboni's drugstore is now in a different building than the one shown in the 1940s photograph.

155. Bruce Arons, interview by author, October 3, 2012.

156. Ibid.

157. Ina Zall Cutler, interview by author, July 30, 2012.

158. Paula Segal Markofksy, interview by author, August 2003.

159. Plymouth County Land Court, 10620, 1932; 13341-3, nonpayment of taxes, 1936; 13747, foreclosure, 1937.

160. PCD: Joseph Sadow to Plymouth Cooperative Bank, foreclosure, 1568: 75, 1929; Sadow to Plymouth Savings Bank, 1644: 395–96, 1933; Brene Greenspoon to Plymouth Coop, foreclosure, 1632: 167, 1932; Cohen

to Plymouth Cooperative Bank, foreclosure, 1630: 411, 1932; Fannie Markus to Plymouth Coop Bank, foreclosure, 1681: 257, 1935.

161. Penn, interview by author.

162. Goldstein, "Plymouth During the Depression," 111–15, 123–29.

163. Rotenberg, interview with author.

164. Congregation Beth Jacob, "Silver Jubilee Program," 6; Toabe, Winokur and Keller, "Founders' Breakfast." Toabe mentioned twenty-four *members* rather than families. Penn, interview by author; *Congregation Beth Jacob 100th Anniversary Tribute Book.*

165. Penn, "Memories of Growing Up," 2–3; Penn, interview with author; Congregation Beth Jacob, "Silver Jubilee Program," 6; *OCM*, "Purim Party Is Enjoyed by Beth Jacob," March 17, 1933; *OCM*, "Yom Kippur Is Observed Here," September 21, 1934; *OCM*, "Elect Officers for the Year," September 11, 1931. *OCM*, "Resnick Boy Confirmed by Rabbi Goldbergh," June 2, 1933.

166. Penn, "Memories of Growing Up," 1–3.

167. Congregation Beth Jacob, "Silver Jubilee Program," 6; Geller, interview by author; *OCM*, "Church Notes," December 17, 1936.

168. Toabe, Winokur and Keller, "Founders' Breakfast"; Winokur and Winokur, interview with author, Vicki Blass Fitzgerald and Ray Russo; *OCM*, "New Rabbi Here Dec. 1," November 1936; *OCM*, "Reception for New Rabbi," December 17, 1936.

169. *OCM*, "Church Notes," June 3, 1937, December 1, 1938, February 16, 1939.

170. Ibid., December 1, 1938; June 23, 1938; February 16, 1939; January 4, 1940; January 18, 1940; August 17, 1939.

171. *OCM*, "Jewish New Year to Be Celebrated Next Week," September 26, 1940; *OCM*, "Yom Kippur Service Starts Next Tuesday," September 25, 1941; *OCM*, "Jewish New Year to Be Solemnized," September 1941; *OCM*, "Yom Kippur Services Start Friday Evening," October 3, 1940.

172. Penn, "Memories of Growing Up," 2; Penn, interview with author.

173. *OCM*, "Church Notes," November 17, 1938, March 9, 1939; *OCM*, "Notes, Beth Jacob Synagogue," May 23, 1938, mentions Mrs. Friedman as the Hebrew teacher.

174. The series of articles on "Life in Palestine" ran in the *OCM* in the first half of 1937. Ina Zall Cutler, interview with author.

175. *OCM*, "Local Jews in Protest," March 31, 1933; *OCM*, "Raise $100 for Jewish Fund," November 3, 1933.

176. *OCM*, "Rabbi Will Lead Union Services," November 17, 1938.

177. Ibid.; *OCM*, December 1, 1938.

178. *OCM*, "Local Minister, Rabbi Speak at Jewish Temple," December 8, 1938; *OCM*, "Church Council Meets at Beth Jacob Synagogue," December 15, 1938.

179. Clark, "Homefront," 137–46.

180. *OCM*, "100 Children Join Rabbi Friedman in 'Thanks' That They Live in America," July 10, 1941.

181. Susanne Taub Dubroff, interview with author, March 28, 2009.

182. CBJ Newsletter, *Michab Chadashot*, October 1941. This rare bit of ephemera was mailed by Rose Sherman Geller to her brother Hyman at Fort Bragg and was found decades later among his papers. *OCM*, "Dr. Policow Back to Dental Office," March 7, 1945.

183. Twenty-one men from Plymouth's Jewish community served in World War II, according to Rose Geller's article in *Congregation Beth Jacob 100th Anniversary Tribute Book*.

184. Rose Geller quoted in Clark, "Homefront," 139.

185. *OCM*, "Meet Death in Boston Fire," December 3, 1942; B. Resnick, personal communication with author, October 21, 2012.

186. Klasky, interview with author; S. Resnick, interview with author.

187. S. Resnick, interview with author; Geller, interview with author, September 9, 2012.

188. *OCM*, "Dr. Duberstein States Policy Relative to Board of Health," February 25, 1937; *OCM*, "Constable," March 7, 1946; Lawrence Winokur, interview with author, October 10, 2012. Reubin Winokur also served as town counsel for Plymouth in the 1970s; Arons, interview with author. Arons was surprised to realize that he was the first Jewish selectman in Plymouth.

189. *OCM*, Obituary, Abraham S. Feinberg, October 1961; *OCM*, "Dr. Waterman Appointed to Hospital Staff," January 19, 1934. A personal communication from James Baker, former historian of the Old Colony Club, October 5, 2012, indicated many more Jewish members than Jewish people in Plymouth today might think.

190. *OCM*, Obituary, Hattie Resnick Waterman.

191. Jackie Keller Winokur, interview with author, October 3, 2012; Arons, interview with author, October 3, 2012. The Beach Club has been inclusive in its membership for many years.

192. *OCM*, "Testimonial Dinner [for Rabbi Friedman]," December 5, 1941; "Contributors to the Final Redemption of the Mortgage of the Beth Jacob Synagogue," manuscript, CBJ archives, March 14, 1944.

193. Raymond Russo, interview with author, October 14, 2012. Kingston Animal Hospital is still in business, run by one of Ray and Millie's sons, Dr. Mark Russo.

194. Congregation Beth Jacob, "Script for 75th Anniversary Program."

195. Ibid.; Toabe, Winokur and Keller, "Founders' Breakfast."

196. Congregation Beth Jacob, "Script for 75th Anniversary Program"; Congregation Beth Jacob, "Founders' Breakfast."

197. Congregation Beth Jacob, "Script for 75th Anniversary Program"; *Congregation Beth Jacob 100th Anniversary Tribute Book.*

198. Rabbi Laurence Silverman, personal communication, October 18, 2012. The congregation sold the Community Center to the Town of Plymouth in autumn of 2012.

Bibliography

Anderson, Robert Charles. "Pilgrim Village Families Sketch: Moses Simonson/Simmons." www.americanancestors.org/pilgrim-families-moses-simonson.

Bacon, Josephine. *The Illustrated Atlas of Jewish Civilization: 1000 Years of History*. London: Quantum Books, Ltd., 2009.

Baietti, Vincent (Jelly). Interview by author. Video recording. Plymouth, MA. August 6, 2002.

Baker, James W. *Images of America: Plymouth*. Charleston, SC: Arcadia Publishing, 2002.

Bangs, Jeremy D. "Moses Simons of Leiden." *New England Ancestors Magazine* 5, no. 3 (2004): 54–55.

———. *Strangers and Pilgrims, Travelers and Sojourners: Leiden and the Foundations of Plymouth Plantation*. Plymouth, MA: General Society of Mayflower Descendants, 2009.

Bartlett, Joan, ed. *Joseph Busi of Plymouth: A Memoir*. Plymouth, MA: Warren Cove Family Histories, 1999.

Bienen, Leigh. "Mayer, Levy." Florence Kelly: 1891–1899. florencekelley.northwestern.edu/legal/lawyers/levymayer.

Bloom, Morris. Interviews by author. Video recording. Plymouth, MA. October 2001 and February 23, 2002.

Bradford, William. *Of Plymouth Plantation, 1620–1647*. With notes and introduction by Samuel Eliot Morison. New York: Knopf, 1952.

Carlisle, Rodney P., ed. *The Jewish Americans.* New York: Facts on File, 2011.

"A Century of Immigration: 1820–1924." From Haven to Home: 350 Years of Jewish Life in America. www.loc.gov/exhibits/haventohome/haven-century.html.

Chaffee, John, ed. *Beyond Plymouth Rock.* Vol. I, *The Ties That Bind.* Plymouth, MA: Plymouth Public Library Corporation, 2002.

Clapp, Edward J. *The Port of Boston: A Study and a Solution of the Traffic and Operating Problems of Boston, and Its Place in the Competition of the North Atlantic Seaports.* New Haven, CT: Yale University Press, 1916. www.gjenvick.com/PortsAndHarbors/Boston1916-CommonwealthPierAsAJointPassengerTerminal.html#axzz2DI2jbiPk.

Clark, Bobbi. "The Homefront 1941–1945." In *Beyond Plymouth Rock.* Vol. I, *The Ties That Bind*, edited by John Chaffee, 137–46. Plymouth, MA: Plymouth Public Library Corporation, 2002.

Cohen, Deborah. Interview by author. Tape recording. Plymouth, MA. April 9, 2005.

Cohen, Harris B. "What Is Cohen's Store." Manuscript, 1965. Courtesy of Deborah Cohen.

Congregation Beth Jacob 100th Anniversary Tribute Book. Plymouth, MA: Congregation Beth Jacob. 2009. www.slideshare.net/generationsweb/cbj100tributebookfinalalt.

Congregation Beth Jacob. "Congregation Beth Jacob Yiddish Ledger Translation, 1909–1916." Translated by Caraid O'Brien, 2008. Congregation Beth Jacob archives.

———. "Script for 75th Anniversary Program." Manuscript, circa 1987. Congregation Beth Jacob archives.

———. "75th Anniversary Program." Plymouth, MA: Congregation Beth Jacob, 1988.

———. "Silver Jubilee Program." Manuscript, 1937. Congregation Beth Jacob archives.

Cutler, Nancy Kabelsky, and Rose Sherman Geller. Interview by author. Audio recording. Plymouth, MA, August 2002.

Dalin, David G., and Jonathan Rosenbaum. *Making a Life, Building a Community: A History of the Jews of Hartford.* New York: Holmes and Meier, 1997.

Davis, William T. *Plymouth Memoirs of an Octogenarian.* Plymouth, MA: Memorial Press, 1906.

Dexter, Henry Martyn, and Morton Dexter. *The England and Holland of the Pilgrims.* Boston: Houghton Mifflin and Co., 1905.

Engstrom, Victoria B. "The Forges of Chiltonville." Pilgrim Hall Museum, 1978. www.pilgrimhall.org/PSNote26.htm.

"European Jewish Emigration via the Port of Hamburg." www1.uni-hamburg.de/rz3a035/emigration.html.

Evans, Nicholas J. "Leaving the Homeland." "Arrival of Passengers." "Arrival in a North Sea Port." *Moving Here: Migration Stories.* www.movinghere.org.uk/galleries/histories/jewish/journeys/journeys.htm.

Fennell, Christopher. "Plymouth Colony Legal Structure." 1998. The Plymouth Colony Archive Project. www.histarch.uiuc.edu/plymouth/ccflaw.html.

"The Fleets, Feeder Lines, Railway Companies." The Ships List. www.theshipslist.com/ships/lines/feeders.html.

Geller, Rose. "A Brief History of Congregation Beth Jacob." In *Congregation Beth Jacob 100th Anniversary Tribute Book.* www.slideshare.net/generationsweb/cbj100tributebookfinalalt.

———. "History of Congregation Beth Jacob." In *Congregation Beth Jacob 75th Anniversary Program.*

———. Interview by author. Video recording. Plymouth, MA. July 2001.

Goldberg, Harvey E. "Life Cycle." Yivo Encyclopedia of Jews in Eastern Europe. www.yivoencyclopedia.org/article.aspx/Life_Cycle.

Goldstein, Karin. "From Pilgrims to Poverty: Biography of an Urban Renewal Neighborhood in Plymouth, Massachusetts." Dissertation, Boston University, 2006.

———. "High School Days." *Plymouth Patch*, June 11, 2011. plymouth.patch.com/articles/high-school-days.

———. "Plymouth During the Depression." In *Beyond Plymouth Rock: America's Hometown in the 20th Century.* Vol. I, *The Ties That Bind,* edited by John Chaffee, 111–15, 123–29. Plymouth, MA: Plymouth Public Library Corporation, 2002.

———. "Plymouth's Jewish Community." In *Beyond Plymouth Rock: America's Hometown in the 20th Century.* Vol. I, *The Ties That Bind,* edited by John Chaffee, 43–45. Plymouth, MA: Plymouth Public Library Corporation, 2002.

Guthrie, Woody. "Suassos Lane." lyrics.wikia.com/Woody_Guthrie:Suassos_Lane.

Hoberman, Michael. *How Strange It Seems: The Cultural Life of Jews in Small-Town New England.* Amherst: University of Massachusetts Press, 2008.

Hunt, Herman. "A 'Spanish Lady' Plagues Plymouth." In *Beyond Plymouth Rock: America's Hometown in the 20th Century.* Vol. I, *The Ties That Bind,* edited by John Chaffee, 69–70. Plymouth, MA: Plymouth Public Library Corporation, 2002.

Imhoff, Sarah. "The Civil War to the Gilded Age 1859–1900." In *The Jewish Americans*, edited by Rodney Carlisle, 39–56. New York: Facts on File, 2011.

JewishGen Communities Database. data.jewishgen.org/wconnect/wc.dll?jg~jgsys~jgcd.

Johnson, Caleb. "Crime and Punishment in the Plymouth Colony." Mayflower History. www.mayflowerhistory.com/History/CrimeAndPunishment.php.

Johnson, Paul. *A History of the Jews*. New York: Harper & Row, 1987.

Jones, G. Lloyd. *The Discovery of Hebrew in Tudor England: A Third Language*. Manchester, UK: Manchester University Press, 1983.

Kaufman, Betty Shoman. Interview by Sandy Kaufman Lipset and Craig Lipset. Video recording. Sands Point, NY. September 1997.

Klasky, Melvin. Interview by author. Video recording. Plymouth, MA. May 1999.

Langdon, George D. *Pilgrim Colony: A History of New Plymouth, 1620–1691*. New Haven, CT: Yale University Press, 1966.

Leibensperger, Summer. "The Colonial Era and the American Revolution: Beginnings to 1783." In *The Jewish Americans*, edited by Rodney Carlisle, 3–20. New York: Facts on File, 2011.

"Liverpool, England—Background to the New Dock, 1895–1913." The Gjenvick-Gjønvik Archives. www.gjenvick.com/PortsAndHarbors/Liverpool/1895-1913-Liverpool-BackgroundToTheNewDock.html#ixzz2AYcBWWbe.

Lothrop's Plymouth (Mass.) Directory. Union Publishing, 1932, 1936.

Masters, Edgar Lee. *Levy Mayer and the New Industrial Era*. Rachel Mayer, 1927. fkdocs.sesp.northwestern.edu/nodes/pages/57325/17397.

Meyer, Isidore. "America's First Thanksgiving." *Contemporary Jewish Record* 2, no. 6 (1939): 9–15.

———. *The Hebrew Exercises of Governor William Bradford*. Plymouth, MA: Pilgrim Society, 1973.

Mills, Maggie. "Supplement." *Old Colony Memorial*. December 10, 2001.

Mills, Maggie, and Rose Sherman Geller. Interview by author. Video recording. Plymouth, MA. August 2002.

National Park Service. "Ellis Island—History." Ellis Island Foundation, Inc. www.ellisisland.org/genealogy/ellis_island_history.asp.

"The Pale of Settlement." Yivo Encyclopedia. www.yivoencyclopedia.org/article.aspx/Pale_of_Settlement.

Penn, Milton. "Memories of Growing Up in Plymouth." Manuscript, 1988. Congregation Beth Jacob Archives.

Pilgrim Tercentenary Pageant 1921 Program. Boston: Southgate Press, 1921.

Plymouth District Telephone Directories. New England Telephone & Telegraph Company, 1942–56.

Raphael, Marc Lee. *The Synagogue in America: A Short History.* New York: New York University Press, 2011.

Resident and Business Directory of Plymouth, Massachusetts. Boston: Union Publishing, 1903–1924

Resnick, Albert. "First Prize Essay." *Plymouth Products* 141 (August–September 1924): 5–7.

Resnick, Bernard. Interview by author. Video recording. Plymouth, MA. August 2002.

Sadow, Sue. *Can Do (Said Sue): A Rich Life Helping the Poor.* Denver: Beaumont Books, 1993.

Sarna, Jonathan D. "The Jews of Boston in Historical Perspective." In *The Jews of Boston*, edited by Jonathan Sarna, Ellen Smith and Scott-Martin Kosofsky, 3–20. Boston: Combined Jewish Philanthropies of Greater Boston, Inc., 1993.

Sarna, Jonathan, Ellen Smith and Scott-Martin Kosofsky, eds. *The Jews of Boston.* Boston: Combined Jewish Philanthropies of Greater Boston, Inc., 1993.

"Ship Descriptions." The Ships List. www.theshipslist.com/ships/descriptions/ShipsC.shtml.

Shurtleff, Nathaniel B., and David Pulsifer, eds. *Records of the Colony of New Plymouth in New England.* Boston: Press of W. White, 1855.

Slutsky, Yehuda. "Pogroms." Jewish Virtual Library. www.jewishvirtuallibrary. org/jsource/judaica/ejud_0002_0016_0_15895.html.

Smith, Ellen. "Israelites in Boston," In *The Jews of Boston*, edited by Jonathan Sarna, Ellen Smith and Scott-Martin Kosofsky, 45–65. Boston: Combined Jewish Philanthropies of Greater Boston, Inc., 2005.

Solem, Borge. "Steerage on Steamships." Norway Heritage: Hands Across the Sea. www.norwayheritage.com/articles/templates/voyages. asp?articleid=28&zoneid=6.

Spiro, Ken. "Pale of Settlement, History Crash Course #56." Aish HaTorah. www.aish.com/jl/h/48956361.html.

———. "WorldPerfect: The Jewish Impact on Civilization." Simple to Remember, Judaism Online. www.simpletoremember.com/articles/a/jewsamerica.

"Steamship Berths Assignment for Foreign Passenger Steamship Lines at Boston Harbor" (1914). Gjenvick-Gjonvick Archives. www.gjenvick.com/PortsAndHarbors/Boston/1914-BerthAssignments-SteamshipLines-BostonHarbor.html#ixzz20BkvECcN.

Suberman, Stella. *The Jew Store*. Chapel Hill, NC: Algonquin Books, 2001.

Toabe, Mitchell, Reubin Winokur and Harry Keller. "Congregation Beth Jacob Founders' Breakfast." Videotaped lecture. October 8, 2000.

Town of Plymouth. *Annual Reports of the Town Officers of the Town of Plymouth.* Plymouth, MA: Avery and Doten, 1880–1945.

Winokur, Adeline, and Reubin Winokur. Interview by author, Vicki Blass Fitzgerald and Ray Russo. Video recording. Plymouth, MA. August 2001

Index

INDEX

V

Vanzetti, Bartolomeo 52
Veddel 26
Verdun, Battle of 98
Vilna 31
Vilna *guberniya* 24
Vilna Shul 129
Vine Hills Cemetery 128

W

Wareham, Massachusetts 55
Waterman, Dr. Isidore (Earl) 103, 108,
    124
Waterman, Hattie Resnick 31, 103, 108,
    123, 124
Waterman, Richard 104, 126
Waterman, Rollene 8, 31, 123
Water Street 44, 63, 81, 88
White Star Line 27, 29
Whitney, Rev. Arthur B. 43
Winokur, Adeline Mankoff 106
Winokur family 105, 124, 129
Winokur, Reubin 81, 103, 108, 109, 113,
    116, 123
Winthrop, John 13
Wirtzburger, Richard 109
Wise, Rabbi Nathan 126, 127
Woolworth Building 87
World War I 58, 72, 74, 83, 96, 97, 98
World War II 60, 101, 102, 119, 123, 124

Y

yacht club 48, 95
Yiddish language 25, 90, 102, 113, 114
Young Judea 114

Z

Zall, Ina. *See* Cutler, Ina Zall
Zall, Jeannette Hurwitz 108, 121
Zall's All-Stars 108, 109
Zall, William 108, 109, 122
Zavalcofsky, Dottie 113
Zavalcofsky family 83, 111
Zitter and Maged 59

About the Author

Karin J. Goldstein, a native of Chicago, fell in love with family history as a child and was always asking older relatives and neighbors about "the old times." After much soul searching about a career, she decided to become a museum curator and moved to Plymouth, Massachusetts, where she has lived since 1992. When the Plymouth Jewish History Project started in 2001, she began researching and continued off and on for more than ten years. Not only has the project given her deeper roots in her adopted community, but it also led indirectly to a dissertation topic on a Plymouth neighborhood. Goldstein has a PhD in American studies from Boston University and works as a museum curator at Plimoth Plantation and as an adjunct professor of history at Bridgewater State University.

Visit us at
www.historypress.net